THE TITAN EQUIVALENT

THE TITAN EQUIVALENT

D. C. RAYMOND

THE LAST CHAPTER

— 1965 —

- First Russian school computer built in Nõo, Estonia.
- I.J. Good speculates that artificial intelligence, via super-intelligent machines designing increasingly intelligent machines, could bring about an "intelligence explosion."
- Gordon Moore discovers that the number of transistors appears to double each year (later amended to two years). Futurists will refer to this as "Moore's Law."
- Seventeen-year-old Ray Kurzweil unveils his first music synthesizer and the song it has composed on the gameshow *I've Got a Secret*.

"Did you get all that, or would you like me to repeat it?," the guide said.

"Uhh..."

The world had ADHD. She needed to think. Sophie let the hustle and bustle of *Polus* port distract her; she'd lost her place in mind. She choked down a dry swallow. She tried not to think about relative speeds, about spin, about departure times, or about how the only thing parting her from certain death were thin sheets of tempered metal spitting in the eyes of God and logic. She decided, instead, to think of how she'd gotten where she stood. It was a bit of a blur. What would the girls back home say?

Marlene was likely still going on about that one time at Six Flags. Years on, she still brought it up whenever opportunity presented. "She'll get all the way up to the head of the line," she'd be saying, "and one toe onto a ship, she'll be running 'wee-wee-wee' all the way home. Just like that time at Six Flags." Six Flags was when they were eight years old, for Christ.

So she didn't like roller coasters. Never could gather why folks liked being scared so much. Life was scary enough without chasing it. This was not a roller coaster—it did not bring you from point A to point B and then back to point A mindlessly; there was a destination. It hadn't been designed to frighten children and left in the care of drug- and hormone-addled teenagers. These engineers were, even if English, more trustworthy than that. And she wasn't eight anymore.

What about Mary? Poor, delicate Mary, the other extreme, scared enough for the entire town. Convinced Sophie had superpowers whenever she called to order takeout, Mary was probably staging a sit-in at her parents' out of "sympathy."

"I just don't get you, sometimes, Sophie. For my *Rumschpringe*, I went to Shreveport. Stayed in the first motel I could find and played games. It sucked."

Sophie laughed, threw her rucksack over her shoulder and said, "Was that the Englishmen's fault, Mare?" but Mary shook it off. Mary had her own language of shakes, nods, shivers, and hunches, a gesture patois in which Sophie was fluent. Most of them, like Inuit words for "snow", conveyed only subtle variations around the same theme: thirty-two flavors of fear or anxiety. This particular, dismissive shake meant reproval, masking fear for a friend's safety. "I watched a bunch of the news reports while I was there. They were all about riots and murder, chaos, still."

"Yes, Mary, news reports *are* all murder and chaos. Do you know what real life isn't?"

"Hm?"

"A news report."

To that, Mary just *shiveled*—that was her house blend of rustling and shivering that meant a 1:1 ratio of disapproval and concern.

Sophie tried, somewhat futilely, to un-shivel her. "Look, I know you think I'm some daredevil, but I'm not—ask anyone, you're literally like the only person less adventurous than me in town. I'm not gonna go off half-cocked or whatever. You've seen my itinerary; you helped me write it. I'm sticking to it. I'm just going to New Wardenclyffe and back. It's not even far."

Of course, she'd never tell Mare the whole truth. She'd made a *version* of the trip plan with her, sure—and that's the one the rest of the village saw, too—but there was another, secret plan she would never share. One to go as far away as the Englishman's technology would take her. Of course, now that she'd put toe to platform (at least at Six Flags she'd gotten up to the ride car—she was ready to scream "wee-wee." It was spite, the strongest of human motivators, that kept her going. Fuck Marlene.

A fear of strange technology and people was only natural, all things considered. For Sophie and her people, this kind of travel was still unknown. She told herself, reminded herself really, how routine these trips had become for the rest of the world. Odds of an accident, she'd been told, were like nothing. Safer than a horse ride. It didn't help. In little under an hour, she'd be leaving solid earth.

The terminal pulsated with businessmen, families, businesswomen, tourists, business...other things. Seemed like gender as a concept kinda exploded at some point. Sophie had trouble telling one person from the next. It soothed her. As a girl who'd been mocked for a masculine voice and interests most of her life, it made her feel a way she'd never realized she'd never felt before: unobserved. No one noticed her at all here. Still, kind of confusing, you know? Back at the mobile floor, she'd asked directions from someone who looked like Cindy Crawford, but sounded like Tom Waits and might've been wearing a tail. She hoped she was just wearing it. On the outside. In the moment, she lost the ability to speak and wandered off. No judgment; she just had to adjust is all. Far as Soph was concerned you could marry a cow if you could prove equivalent consent.

"Now boarding Group zero-one-A for skimmer bound to Tacitus

Station at Gate six-five-seven. Group zero-one-A for skimmer bound for Tacitus Station. Gate six-fifty-seven."

Sophie checked her ticket—no one else had one like hers: paper. They sent an old man to the back to get the printer just for her people, the Amish, and Mennonites, none of which she guessed came through much.

Jack—Jack was the old man's name, by far the most ordinary name she'd encountered—fiddled with it, but even he seemed to be probing some kind of alien technology until he found a *switch*.

Devices didn't seem to have those anymore. Things just sort of "knew" when you wanted them on. Her copy of *A Young Lady's Illustrated Rumspringa Almanac* (a flat, matte black thing with a screen that seemed like paper but moved with a touch and lit up when she looked at it) assured her this was well within guidelines and had no psychographic components. Sophie figured they just read body language, knew where your eyes went or whatever. Maybe the face right before turning something on was basically the same for everyone, that sort of thing.

Either way, switch *found* had been only half the battle. In the end Sophie had to explain how to "flip" it, and "plug" the wire into the dusty, unused port on their terminals. All this stuff had been re-invented and re-installed after the Derealization, according to the Almanac, specifically for the Boylish. It printed out in hazy turquoise, a bright pink stripe down the center. "Need to replace your ink ribbon or cartridge," she said. They stared at her as a dog might stare at the Olympics.

She nodded and smiled, and took her ticket here, to the hologram info desk "person," a mock-up of Amelia Earhart best Sophie could tell, and had been here ever since, listening to science she barely comprehended. The explanations, for her, may as well have been a wizard explaining how to turn soup into gold with the delicate application of precision spitting. Still, she'd picked up Japanese just from her grandpa repeating things often enough and her wanting to communicate with him so badly. Maybe that could work with Quantum Physics? Yeah. Right. And monkeys might fly out of her butt.

"Did you get all that, or—"

"Shut up for a second," Sophie said, and Amelia stopped talking.

She listened for the boarding call. Group 47-B. Plenty of time still to be confused.

"Are you quite finished, Emmex[1]?"

"Excuse me?" Sophie turned. Some sort of dumpy creature of indeterminate sex but determinate school librarianity, they wore one of those faces like Sophie owed late fees of some sort, possibly a bridge toll?

"Are you done with the gram? I need to find terminal four." Sophie swore their breath smelled musty.

"It's next to terminal three, dude. Ma'am. You. ...Look I'm Boylish so it's gonna be a second."

"Yeah, okay," they said, and wandered off mumbling, "Cucking tourists."

"I'm not sure what that means but it sounds bad!" She turned back for another round of science. The light on her face had gone out as she'd reveled. She waved her hand, but before she'd actually gestured, Amelia reappeared, Cheshire-smile-first. "Whoa! That's an old-fashioned ticket you've got there!" she said, as if Sophie had just walked up. "My Alpha[2] says it's printed with ink on tree pulp or 'paper,' which means its fabricators must be from either a Mormon or Boylish community. Would you mind telling me which?" It waited there for a response in what for the first time Sophie noticed was a small animation loop. It would've sat there for eternity without breaking its customer service smile if she never answered.

"Uh...Boylish," she said, releasing it from its perdition.

For a half-second, Amelia's face stuttered. Then, "Ah, that makes this easy-peas." She leaned in and affected a whisper, "The Mormons're a little more secretive and anti-science since the Derealization." Amelia stood back up. "You must be on *Rumspringa*."

"Yeah-yeah, just get to explaining the thing I'm getting on again."

A small animation cycle, just a tad unnatural. "The Stream Rail?" Amelia said as if repeating Sophie. "I can tell you all about it! It's the essence of what I said years ago: 'Never do things others can do and will do, if there are things others cannot do or will not do.' I'll do my best to explain it in your low-tech vocabulary, Miss—" her lips blurred a bit as it filled in the name "–Higgins. Are you familiar with the concept of quantum entanglement?" She lifted her head slightly as if waiting for the answer. Sophie let the animation cycle again. It was fascinating how lifelike and yet not they'd managed to make these holograms. She reached out and "touched" Amelia's cheek—her fingers passed through—and felt the tingle of electrons resisting one another's caress.

Sophie shook it off. What was the question?

"Are you familiar with the concept of quantum entanglement?" Amelia repeated in the exact same intonation and rhythm as before.

"Uh, yeah. Two particles or whatever that act the same."

"At a 20c level of understanding, yes. Two particles, once entangled, act in unison across vast distances–perhaps over any distance. You may have heard it called the relativity barrier loophole. It's what the rail system operates on."

Behind her, a screen Sophie had thought was a map of the solar system zoomed into Earth, past a complex satellite system with streams of light coursing between them. It stopped when it reached the station she was currently aboard, *Polus*, where it slowed to a crawling approach. "The mastery of quantum fields in the late 21st Century, much like the Black Algorithm and the subsequent mass derealizations it caused at the beginning of that same century, changed all fields of study. We came to see travel through space as less of sailing or flying from point A to point B and more like skipping a stone along the surface of localized time phenomena. Use of entanglement and super-positioning made communication instantaneous, remote repairs possible, and travel faster than light–because 'travel' wasn't really happening, not the way we used to conceptualize it." A pause. "Did you get all that or would you like me to repeat it?"

"Go on," Sophie said, though she most definitely had not gotten it.

"Through a long process using standard interstellar travel, sometimes over generations, mechanical drones lay a spiral 'track' of entangled electrons between destinations, beginning and ending with a single 'row' of super-positioned electrons. Once laid, an entangled vessel can exist at both ends simultaneously and then come to a rest on the opposite side of the track rather than its original location. From an outside perspective, the trip is instantaneous. From within the ship, because of several variables, individual experience may vary. I'm just a pilot, so all this spooky science racks my little brain. I'm assured, though, it's not only safer than flying, but is statistically the safest way to travel mankind has ever invented."

Replaying this had not helped at all.

"Did you get all that, or would you like me to repeat it?"

JUBILEE STATION, for Sophie, resembled, closest, the pictures she'd seen of old Las Vegas. That's why she'd chosen it. All synthetic colors like purple, hot pink, and that golden yellow only neon lights give off. All of it aroused her in the oddest way.

There were two thousand passengers—patrons? What should she call people on a space station-casino-hotel-transport hub? Customers? *Tourists*—there were two thousand tourists aboard *Jubilee*. At any rate, they bustled. Right past each other, most as if they didn't even sense the others, some noticing one another too much—either damn-near doing it on the floor or getting into fist fights to prove they didn't want to do it with each other. Eventually, a station agent would arrive, tell them to go get a room for that kind of crap, or at very least a prostitution booth. There, drenched in yellow light and surrounded by four walls of controllable transparency, one could fight or fuck to their heart's content, professional partners vended upon request.

Sophie couldn't decide whether it all was decadence or progress, civilization's end or its beginning. She just knew she hadn't stopped being aroused at any moment. That's why she ran to her room.

Inside, the room and its plainness—real walls, not see-thru, bookshelves, chairs, and beds—at first comforted her, but as she attempted to sit on a chair or lay on the bed, she found them just strange enough to remind her how alien she was, that this world was to her.

The chair was too comfortable: it felt as if she bent her knees, weightlessly in space; the armrests pointed inward at an exceptionally natural angle, each with half a QWERTY layout and buttons on the sides. The keys were flat and just barely depressed when she touched them, with almost no pressure applied. The back and headrest took the exact shape of a spine and kept her in perfect posture without any effort on her part, like an old mother giant cupped you in her hand.

The bed felt like a womb.

She decided she'd sleep on the chair, for fear the bed would make her question her original decision, all those years ago, to emerge into this toilet of a world, and, perhaps convince her to never, ever wake up again. The chair like antigravity cradled her so that it took only minutes to drift away.

UNTIL, that is, the rudest of all of nature's hullabaloos startled her awake. Her eyes popped open.

Was this one of those lucid dreams? Yeah. Had to be. If so, she needed to wake up. The room of soft hell had some misguided white noise generator to help her sleep that some insane English had set to "cicada" because they grew up in space, the only explanation for being comforted by such a sound. Asleep, she only dreamed the actual cicada on the coffee table across from her, next to the bed.

She'd always hated those tone-deaf, arrhythmic assholes. How and why was it that they refused to let their "songs" fall into a pattern of any sort? Every time you adjusted to it, it changed. What kind of absolute psychopath would choose to sleep to this?

She squeezed her eyes shut and peeled them open. Nothing. She went into the bathroom, and once she realized how to activate the faucet (putting her hands toward the spigot), she ran it to try to get herself to pee, because she would wake up to go to the bathroom if she had to pee. She finished actually peeing though, not something she could ever do in a dream.

Realizing she wouldn't be waking up anytime soon, her hatred rose in her throat, hot and acidic like bile. She poured herself to standing out of the cloud-like chair. She scanned her peripheral view for weapons; her central vision, meanwhile, targeted that shit-bastard fiddler in the other corner of the room, who seemed if not oblivious to her revulsion then arrogantly still in its presence. Her hand found purchase on something—strange, a newspaper seemed as anachronistic as Sophie herself, and, she supposed, the cicada, but dreams had never been accused of following any kind of civilized rules—and she lifted it like a Louisville Slugger, rolled up in accordance with historical customs.

She crept closer. The cicada was, she decided, firmly in the "arrogantly still" column. There was no way his beady little compound eyes hadn't spied her by now; she was within feet.

She tried to slither sideways like a snake. She feigned oblivious ennui like a cat. She stole a glance. They locked eyes. Sophie pounced. The paper made a cracking *clap!*, but also a *crunch* that wasn't the *crunch* she'd anticipated. She reopened her eyes—she had closed them for the execution, incapable of stomaching the demise of even her sworn enemy—to find her paper had *cracked* upon impact, sending the words and newsprint hue away and leaving behind a malfunctioning, rolled up, transparency of unknown composition. A spark flew, and a puff of purple smoke. It felt like paper! What was this magic? She touched it, as if her left hand's reporting couldn't be trusted until her right hand corroborated. It was real. So why did it pass through the cicada as if it were a ghost? Also, it wasn't a cicada. She always mixed that up. It was a fucking grasshopper. Ugh.

On that thought, the lights blinked.

Then again.

Sophie heard the faint murmur of an alarm reverberate in the hall. Another grasshopper landed on the bed. "Fucking gnarly!" she said, and tossed the rolled up screen at it, to similar lack of effect.

The door opened itself and Sophie's ears rang with the unmuffled shriek of the alarm. Reprieve: the door shut. Then again, open. The lights continued to flicker, a-rhythmic and annoying, just like the cicada symphony which grew louder as the moments passed.

She timed her steps and *grande jetéed* through the doorway before it slid shut again.

A SCREAM. To the left, a man tumbled past at the far end where another corridor intersected, swatting at a swarm of holographic grasshoppers swarming around his face. Not grasshoppers. Locusts. When grasshoppers acted like this, they were locusts. Gross. She started to turn, but noticed the high ceilings leaking a dark red, leaving large drip lines on the walls. The liquid was thin and thick at the same time in the way that only bodily fluids could be.

To the right, demanding, a rising cacophony like the locusts' song, but more baritone and chaotic. She hesitated. She turned. The noise rose. A green-black cloud blotted out the hallway as it tumbled unnaturally, involuntarily her way.

Shit! Something hit her shoulder. Cracked on the floor, a chunk of ice like a broken golf ball a few feet from her toes. It was *hailing?* Indoors. In space.

Ribbets. The sound, it was *ribbeting,* the panicked song of a hundred thousand frogs fuck that's what it is fuck it's frogs oh my god that's disgusting—she turned around. The viscous, wet amphibious choir approached. Had to get back into the room with the locusts. Now.

Then something cold, round, and hard struck her temple, and the room shrank into red stars and everything went purple, then purple went black.

"'Grace appears purest in that human form which has either no consciousness or an infinite one, that is, in a puppet or in a god.'

"'Therefore,' I said, somewhat bewildered, 'we would have to eat again from the Tree of Knowledge in order to return to the state of innocence?'

"'Quite right,' he answered. 'And that's the last chapter in the history of the world.'"

—HEINRICH VON KLEIST, "ON THE
MARIONETTE THEATRE"

CHAPTER 1
THE MIGHTY EMBRYO

— 1973 —

- Charles H. Bennett demonstrates general-purpose computation can be performed by a logically and thermodynamically reversible apparatus, or a reversible Turing Machine.

— 1974 —

- Ray Kurzweil founds Kurzweil Computer Products, Inc. and develops a reading machine to allow blind people to understand written text by having a computer read it aloud. This device requires the invention of two enabling technologies: the CCD flatbed scanner and the text-to-speech synthesizer.

— 1980 —

- Paul Benioff publishes a paper describing a quantum mechanical model of Turing machines based on Bennett's work, initiating the field of Quantum Computing.

A rose, maybe. Yeah. Eh. No... Technically, perhaps? Ianus ran out of fucks. He had to admit to himself that it, whatever it was, was beautiful. "Be dead soon," he said. "That's authenticity for you."

"In comparison to what?" said a voice behind Ianus. He recognized that Ionian, received accent. Sister Burr.

"You about to quote me some inspirational tosh? 'Cause I think I may sick up all over your sandals there." He looked her in her hood. The only part of her smugly humble face he could make out was her trademark smirk just beneath the line of the brown cloth.

In the distance, the low, reverberant chants of the other monks seeped into him like therapeutic steam, threatened to take away Ianus' righteous bitterness and sway him into the kind of nap children dread and adults keen over. He turned his ear toward it out of spite to his own cynicism, listened a little harder.

"Walk with me, brother," he heard Burr say, "to the calefactory."

"I'm not your brother, Burr. Just another sinner with delusions of mediocrity."

"There can be no firmer brotherhood, Brother Anaximander."

Ianus lacked the energy to fight or debate her, and she knew it. He'd gone through enough of these back-and-forths with her that his body started skipping straight to exhaustedly giving in to her demands. He nodded.

They walked through an ornately columned cloister encasing a beatific garden fed by reflected starlight. They passed statues of 'Ypatia, of Simone de Beauvoir, and of course one of the sur- half of Ianus' craft name, like some disgruntled Santa Claus holding a list of only the naughty.

▭

They entered the warming room; a single log burned lonely in the hearth. A dozen other monks, brothers and sisters both, worked finger-paint equations on a wall twelve feet high, three of the monks on ladders. Ianus cast a casual glance at the mural but couldn't make heads or tails of it. Dyscalculia made numbers float in the air and soften as he tried to grasp them, like dreams upon waking. It's why Ianus couldn't be a Chaos Monk and had to work in the manipulation and interpretation of metaphor exclusively. Only the ambidextrous monks could waltz between allegory and equation, logic and irony, twirl them all to see the true past in the dance, and predict the future with flexible precision.

Sister Burr took a seat by the fire and gestured for Ianus to sit across.

"They're working on predicting the Dragon's Knee."

"I seem to remember that being unpredictable."

"To a large degree, yes; it is a complex system and resists prediction. But predicting human behavior in macro is simpler than one may think once she comprehends how the oracles work. We can predict the behavior of human organizations, which behave archetypally, to within a few years. Individuals are much more complex than groups. Well, apart from fascists."

"You can say that twice."

"You are troubled, brother," Burr said.

"No shit," Ianus said.

"Any would be."

It offered little comfort. Just focus on the fire. His eyes warmed; his vision blurred. He wiped; tears wet his fingertips. Not enough. Grief sent his humanity underground; he grew more mechanical by the moment. "Last night I dreamt of robot men, machines without pity, stomping through a garden and sorting each molecule. Two piles: Ones or Zeroes. But as they tore each One from the ground, they found it became a Zero, till there were nothing left to murder." Past the Fibonacci spirals of his fingerprints, Burr sat, patience infinitum. Monks had a way of listening, pensive and deep, that made a body feel wrapped up in a blanket a million miles from the thunder. Burr, the eldest of them, listened even deeper, until you relaxed so completely, watching her hear you, that you remembered all the dark, secret things you kept even from yourself. That's when you started to ask the real questions. "Sister."

"Yes."

"What *is* fascism?"

"I'm sure you were taught this, Brother Anaximander."

He searched every shelf. Barren. "Do you have any booze?"

Sister Burr tilted her head back. "Ianus, this is a monastery." She smiled. "Of course we have booze." She raised a hand. A young monk by the door left the room in a hurry, presumably to fetch some alcohol. "To answer your question: fascism is a black algorithm. A memetic virus. A radioactive, malfunctioning idea birthed by recurrent logical fallacy and carried on the cognitive dissonance of an era. In other words: it's bad magic."

"So what's the fallacy?"

"The fallacy *is* logic. Mysticism must precede *and* follow logic. Perception begins in the body with sensation, including emotion. It proceeds to thought, linguistics, rationalizations, logic, and then returns to the body as emotional reaction and physical action. You do not think, 'I'll take a sip of this whiskey,' and then do it. You move to do it *as* you think, 'I'll take a sip of this whiskey.'"

On cue, the younger monk laid a tray of whiskey before them. Ianus grabbed a glass and plucked two cold stones of formerly volcanic ash into it. He poured a double. His hand shook as he lifted the glass. The stones jangled. He shut his eyes and focussed on his breath until the jangling eased. "What in fumbling virgin fuck does the *corpus callosum* have to do with fascism?" He drank.

She smiled with a monk's patience. "To begin an idea with logic is to coldly, blandly divide, for the parts of your brain that use logic must categorize, can only categorize. End of the day, logic is just a high level version of sorting. Once you've squashed into a hierarchy, and all hierarchies are pyramid schemes, the mystical significance that follows you will project onto decisions already made. What part of the psyche do you think made those decisions?"

Ianus put down his damn glass. "I'm out of whiskey, and it's shitey Bourbon and it tastes like bananas. This is Io, not Kentucky. Get some Irish, would ya?"

"The subconscious, full of repressed urges and shadows. That's who made the decisions of how people get categorized."

"Oh. Yeah. That, right."

"The following step is then back to logic, which forms its rationales with cold detachment. 'We decided the Such-and-such people had the least to offer, and that resources were low, or must be since we're all starving, and we feel we, the So-and-so people, are at the top of the hierarchy, which can only be because we are special, and now that we know we are special and the Such-and-suches are a drain on us, getting rid of them is the next logical step. It's only rational."

"The alternative being?"

"Starting with feeling, sensing, observing. With humble awe, a lack of ego, and respect for mystery. *Mysticism.* When we live in our ignorance rather than deny it, we observe without prejudice. Early astronauts called it the Overview Effect. When you see Earth from space for the first time, the world is revealed anew. That everything you ever knew and ever desired is contained on a fragile speck of a spaceship, hanging in the void, with only a thin atmosphere created by centrifugal forces standing between it and annihilation. We *observe* that the world is unknowable, that we are small and can never see it all at once. All at once, it becomes obvious: resources are low because the fearful refuse to share; all people are people and equal to one another when you look them in the eye; we are, the all of us, mortal in a universe where merely being alive is statistically impossible, and that should bind us in co-misery. Then, when reason and logic come, they do so with purpose: divide and label and categorize the *resources*, so that they may be distributed with efficiency and let not a one go hungry. Then we return to the body, where the hand tears the bread in its cupboard and passes it to its neighbor. To begin with the mystic is to sense the world around us and feel the pressures of the world push and pull one another. To know that all is chaos is to be freed from the need to control it, to use reason to find the reasons, explain and explore solutions, and then finally to use the empathy brought from knowing we are tiny and we are alone and we swim together in chaos to resolve the problem. This is compassionate wisdom and advances the all of us in all directions."

Ianus nodded. He knew she was right, but he could no longer feel it. Just as the tears on his cheek were there, but he had not felt the shiver that produced them. "I fear I drift in the wrong direction."

"Grief," she said, and for a moment, seemed as though she would leave it at that. She looked into the fire, so that it flickered in her English eyes. She sighed, and Ianus thought she recalled some loss of her own just then, though what it was he could not fathom. He knew her more then, though—he supposed, he knew them all anew, now. He looked around. What griefs made monks of the maths? He understood now. Everyone here was at an eternal wake. "Grief, guilt, and defensiveness often make us skip to step two, as a way of avoiding the hell of a grief that refuses to abate. Grief is loss, it is regret, it is guilt, it is depression, it is sadness, it is despair. It is overwhelming, and the fear of it, that is the path to mechanism. Fascism, as it was known in 20c. You must fight to stay present, Ianus. Face your grief. Own your shadows. The only way out of grief is through. To run from it is to deify it."

The young monk re-entered, this time with a scroll under his arm instead of a refill. The kid stepped up to Ianus and held out the scroll.

"Okay," Ianus said, "but it better not be Bourbon." He pressed a button on the scroll's handle and the flexparch appeared to write itself.

"Looks like an assignment," Sister Burr said.

"Thank the Maths, as one o' you wankers might say."

Sister Burr released a chuckle. "We prefer to thank the Initial Conditions. Is this good news? Do you feel ready to re-enter the world, Ianus?"

"'Tis a relief, I suppose. Much as I do not anticipate loving melding among the riffraff, I'll be glad for a distraction."

"Just remember what I said, Ianus. You may have to let the emotions in if you're to see clearly."

Ianus nodded and left to retrieve his real clothes from the sanctuary.

▭

SKIMPADS WERE DIFFICULT. She haunted them all, defying reason. Sat at the terminal for his departing skim, in a chair like a cloud, beside a man who smelled of sewer on a planet that pissed perfume, Ianus' choices were her or the present.

He remembered her hair. It was dark, black to the passerby, in truth brown where the light coursed through, like worn leather creases. It hung like posh drapes to her chin and cut up the line of her jaw.

It's not that *Polus* possessed any particular resonance. Not for Ianus, not for anyone. An early model station, it had been fresh out of the

Derealization. It took a generation before fully creative human beings would be grown and capable. The survivors of the Derealization had lingering symptoms, and could do only mash-ups of previous designs. *Polus* reminded Ianus of *Atocha* in Madrid or any of the large train houses still standing, with their large green spaces at center. It had an aviary at its heart, brimming with huge oaks to help filter CO_2 and fend off cabin fever. The walls were large triumphal arches opening onto the various pads, on them the stationary ships that traversed lightyears. The totality similar to a head house at a train station, but in the shape of an almost circle, almost spiral dome, all dictated by gravitational, astrological, and quantum equations. The mid-period stations, from the 2100s, were each works of technological, living art, the nanotech walls inhaled vacuum and breathed in oxygen as you coursed through their hearts. The first Wonders of Off-World.

Above *Polus'* arches, sculpture murals regaled the history of humanity in space in gorgeous relief, reminiscent of the Sistine ceiling, only about things that actually occurred. Sputnik, Laika the Cosmonaut Dog, Yuri Gagarin, the Apollo missions and first Luna landing and Mars Rovers. The Zhang Skim Engine test. But statues in and of themselves were favored among the Reactive.

It was the smell. All these stations smelled the same, despite the flora, despite the humanity or perhaps because of it, definitely because of the attempts to change the smell. Sweat and ozone and deodorizing sprays lackadaisically spritzed about in the pathetic attempt to undo the smell of theoretical things. And the scent, much like the skims, took him places he'd rather not go. But he had to skim for work, and to stay ahead of the grieving he had to work, so in order to escape the memory he had to live within the reminders. The Order had prescribed Io to help him, but nothing worked like work. But for the damned smell between jobs.

He looked around. Trogs floor to ceiling. NPCs grinding their way through somnambulant existences. Slowly but surely, the uniform suit encroached in at the edges of the individuality of normal dress. At the other edge, extremity of overcompensation for the loss of soul. It all seemed so hopeless. Overhead, the departures and returns scrolled next to the gram of Howard Hughes, smiling. Ianus read his ticket.

What a bag of shite.

Another time, the public treated the Order with more respect. A Bowman launching coach for this type of assignment would have been unheard of. Nowadays, the coach ticket was a veritable boon.

Bad timing had dictated the tone of Ianus' life for the most part. Born too early for the Second Romance. Too late for New Renaissance. When he finally came of smoking age, marijuana fell out of favor for public consumption. He struck a match and lit up anyway. The law had not yet caught up with the fashion of the day. Besides, the way his timing went lately, he needed something to dull life's rusty, gangrene-inducing edges. He caught a few stares. Fuck 'em.

The O.B.W.'s star faded a few years hence now. It had done such a good job Romanticizing, the pendulum necessarily swung back toward Reformation. He'd of course argued that the Order had subdivided for the express fucking purpose of preventing reformer splinter cells from arising. They'd of course reminded him that cycles behaved in neither preventable nor re-creatable manners, but may tarry if distracted. The Order staved off division by incorporating it, but the pendulum always swings inexorably from Asymmetrical Design back to Systemic Entropy. They'd been delaying just such a swinging what, seven years now, as they prepared. Only a matter of time fore a Black Swan came long to cash in all that paranoia.

So Ianus found himself in fucking coach. The flight's instantaneous nature did not matter; the spirit of the thing wriggled beneath his skin. Entanglement got chancey out toward the far ends of the ships. Who knows how long it'd take from his perspective, or what he'd have to endure? Memories, strange entities out of a peyote nightmare, an out-of-body experience?

"...Now boarding group four-seven," the attendant-gram said in a tone that told Ianus she'd said it at least twice.

▭

THE DIVINELY INOFFENSIVE, George Harrisonesque voice of the gram stewardess droned on as Ianus found his seat. Her level of physical attractiveness was similarly described: divinely inoffensive,

Harrisonesque. *Spectrum of life now boarding,* she said, *the navigator has turned on the Faraday Harness light. If you haven't already done so, please stow any loose items in the zip pouch on the back of the seat in front of you. Please take your seat and affix your gravity harness...*

Ianus pulled his harness, something like a copper life preserver vest, down until it clicked.

As if cued by Ianus' captive sensation, a nasal voice said, "These flights are bananas, right?"

The girthy creature attached to it proved quantum tunneling as a concept when he kneaded himself into the seat to Ianus' side. It stuck out its hand.

"Mm," Ianus said, hoping that would end it but intuiting he had just egged the conversation on somehow.

"Here one sec, there the next," he said. "Where ya from, buddy?"

"Terra," Ianus said.

"Splains your accent."

"I suppose."

...next to an emergency handle, please read carefully the special instructions card...

"Ooh, big responsibility," the idiot said, incapable of maintaining a subject matter regarding someone not himself.

To Ianus's left, the emergency handle beckoned, sultry. He took it in hand. He thought about pressing the button just to get out of the fucking conversation.

...do not wish to perform the functions described in the event of an emergency, please ask an Stewart to reseat you.

Ianus lifted his hand. Not a Stewart in sight.

"Me," the exomoon of a man continued, "I'm from Venus. Spent most my life mining CO2."

"Lovely. Thank you for your service. I'm gonna try to get a quick nap in before the trip, so..."

If you have any questions about our trip today, please don't hesitate to ask one of your Stewarts. Thank you.

The only evidence that he was the one speaking was the bounce of his combed moustache. "Yeah they run all these ships on diamonds, y'know? Thousands of diamonds. Mine those from Venus atmo, then ship 'em to colonies, terra, and luna nuke plants. They use 'em to absorb the waste, see? That radiation powers the skims. They say each diamond has safely stored power for thousands of years. But each ship needs a ton of em and they keep making more ships and stations and whatnot, so it keeps the lights on. I been powering skims my whole life but never been on one."

A blonde woman with no pores and large eyes stepped into the center of the vessel's dome. Her image transposed to several grams out near the edges where Ianus and his travel-mate sat. "Spectrum of life aboard, I will be your lead Andy this trip. On behalf of Navigator Sanders and all the Quartermasters, welcome aboard Terra Firm Railways wave 777, instant transfer service from *Polus* Station to *Tacitus-Over-Tau*." She smiled with teeth like dentures: too white, too straight, too symmetrical. "Please keep in mind that while every calculation has been done to exacting specification, quantum spin is impossible to predict. While you will be safe at all times, and travel will be instantaneous from the outside, your personal experience of spacetime may vary."

"Do you know how to—"

Ianus sighed. "Just pull it down, man."

He did so. After jostling and molesting his breasts against its will, the harness clicked in. "Oh. Easy enough. So yeah, I wouldn't ever have seen the stars, it weren't for Space Org."

Shit. He's one of those. "Shit. You're one o' those."

"What? What's wrong with Scientology?"

"Nothing if you want to continue worshipping the fucking sun. But hey, whatever gets you out of the house." Ianus closed his eyes.

At this time, make sure your seat backs and tray tables are in their full upright position and that your Faraday Harness is correctly fastened. Also, your cybernetics must be set to 'quantum' mode until an announcement is made upon arrival. Thank you.

"Well! I mean. What do you believe in, then?"

"Chaos. The only truth."

"At this time, any and all cybernetics must be set to 'quantum' mode until an announcement is made upon arrival. If you have any questions, please don't hesitate to ask one of our gram Stewarts. We wish you all an enjoyable skim. Quartermasters, prepare for wave collapse please. Andies, please take your seats for wave collapse."

A high-pitched squeal rose into the air. Ianus' hairs stood on end. The cage around the dome of the vessel lit up like a Tesla sphere. He enjoyed his seat mate's confused face as the current absorbed all light, and they vanished.

SHIT. He stood. The spaceport. Not *Polus. The* spaceport. He looked around, then up overhead. The Terra Firm logo shined down like an evil sun.

It almost bored him at this point. He shouldn't have tried so hard to push the memory from his mind. It's only natural quantum weirdness would lay him here for the duration of the wave.

He walked the platform until he saw. There! Descending the escalator to the pad. Only a few months ago, yet so young. Still what passed for happy in his life. Innocent, more so than now in a million-million ways. Flowers in hand. God, what was up with his hair? How did he think he was pulling that off? He'd cut most of it at the monastery, thank the maths. And the *clothes*. It was like he'd been a different person —only months ago, a different person.

Ianus blinked and lost himself—the backdrop shifted. He spun on heel. Then, there he was: outside, pacing and searching the cab stands futilely. Attempting small talk with a stranger on the curb, like that annoying Scientologist. Oblivious to the fact that the poor man just wanted to catch his cab. The rerun of it bored Ianus to tears. He turned to take in the scenery, maybe catch a glimpse of someone, anyone, anything else.

The station's analog clock—back in vogue, one of those modernist symptoms of the Knee—had broken, its second hand seizing near the three. Was that real or a symptom of his warped perspective?

"Oi," a voice said. Ianus turned. He was standing in someone's way. How was he standing in someone's way? He wasn't really there. He stood inside a memory—the universe's memory—of a moment he'd lived through. The young man before him seemed vaguely familiar.

The intensity in his eyes spoke volumes: he seemed a man without history, a man born adolescent to a world owned by old men corrupted and dying; he held no beliefs dear and nothing had ever been sacred to him. Or, that's what it said to Ianus. The young man's hair he'd dyed tangerine orange two inches ago, and spiked it with gel, from the look, at some point earlier in the week. His clothes young, but—

"Oi!" He pushed Ianus back a foot. "Outta the way, geez." Tangerine walked on. He pulled out something white and lit it aflame with an antique lighter: a *cigarette*. Tangerine was not of this time, either. A door opened to Tangerine's left. His past self entered. Could he see him as well? He looked for Tangerine, but the boy was gone.

Ianus watched himself come back inside. Watched his face fall, from the outside now, as the realization, the gravity of what was happening, hit him. He watched himself know, all at once, that she was gone.

In the corner of his eye, the silhouette of a dark man in a dark coat flickering near baggage claim.

▭

LIKE SURFACING, the oxygen of the present rushed into Ianus's gasping mind. Back aboard the skimmer, at Tacitus, the closest rail station to Jubilee. Thank the Maths the dream hadn't made it to the next part.

...life aboard, welcome to Tacitus-Over-Tau Skimpad. TEST aboard the station is 16:35. AQI aboard is currently 53, so sensitive passengers may want to apply a mask while filtration systems are updated.

For your safety and comfort, please remain seated with your harness affixed until the Navigator turns off the Harness light. This will indicate that our wave has fully collapsed at the Tacitus and that it is safe for you to move about and to activate any cybernetics.

Please check around your seat for any personal belongings you may have brought on board with you and please use caution when opening the overhead bins, as atomic structures may have shifted during the trip. For the next twenty-four hours, you may experience some decoherence lag may occur. Effects include deja vu, or the feeling that you are inside a memory, and what is colloquially referred to as the Mandela Effect—the idea that things were somehow different before your trip. These feelings will fade as you finish collapsing over the next day.

If you require disembarkation assistance, please remain in your seat until all other passengers have disembarked. An Andy will then be pleased to assist you.

On behalf of Terra Firm Railways and the entire crew, I'd like to thank you for joining us on this trip and we are looking forward to seeing you on board again in the near future. Have a nice evening!

Despite instantaneous transportation across the galaxy, limits to travel still existed. Twelve semi-inhabitable planets, moons, meteors, and orbital stations drifted through Tau Ceti's system. While inevitably the Firm would get around to it, the sheer amount precluded spending the time and energy laying electron twixt each and every one of them.

In any case, Jubilee Floating City would never be accessible by skim —their independence and distance from the rail were the biggest draws for criminal enterprises and those fancying their privacy. Ianus would have to take a shuttle from the skim pad to the station.

Had the seat to his left always been empty? Wasn't there...someone? Something about diamonds, the... Ianus shook his head.

ALL OF THESE fucking new stations near the edge smelled *and* looked the same. Say what you will about the Sol stations and their desperate, somewhat naive "unique personal expressions", they had been works of art, so excited by new technology the architects had been, and by finally being invited to design for space, all in the middle of a new Romance.

Now Ianus found himself at the tail end of that Romance. Revolutionary biomimetic architecture now devolved into bones, bones, just bone stations with fucking osteoporosis. Long overdue for a Reformation, the former Romantics incorporated their Reformer proteges' ideas into each new model—boring and uninspired, yet somehow more self-obsessed than their predecessors conscious self-expression. As time wore on, the students tired of playing along. Designs grew lackluster and mechanical. Consistency gradually edged out surprise, prediction overtook experience. The key to maintaining balance during a cusp like the Dragon's Knee was knowing to ignore what people *said* they were doing and pay attention to what they actually *accomplished*. The ends over the means.

The octagonal information kiosk jutted floor to ceiling, resembling a column. The hologram attendant—another example of the literalization of a tenet. The teachings of the Bowmen officially denounced the lack of human interaction in transactions of any sort. After the Derealization, the automated systems were removed by the thousands, replaced by real people. Now, the Reformers replaced real people with holograms of real people. Following the letter of the law as it were—in other words, interpreting the rule literally—accomplished the opposite of the spirit of the law, which was to reinvigorate our lives. Now, they'd gone a step further: boutique holograms. The woman working this kiosk was 21C pop star Marigold Wilson-Carter. Her purple hair flickered in the aged yellow lighting of the station.

"How can I help you today, Mr. Anaximander?"

Shut up. "Can I talk to a person, please?"

"I *am* a person, Mr. Anaximander. Marigold Wilson-Carter composed and sang over forty-seven top ten hits, utterly revitalizing the purchasing of music and ending the streaming era."

"I want someone with a fucking pulse, ye algorithmic kent! Feck's sake. Bowman override!"

She just kept that infernal smile. Unshakable, these hollow bastards. "We apologize, but we don't have any Fleshbuds available at the moment. This station is remote and has difficulty maintaining human staff. Is there anything a gram assistant can help you with?"

Ianus sighed. He composed himself. "Where's my luggage?"

"Your baggage has been safely stowed in the next available shuttle to Jubilee Floating City."

"How long till departure?"

"We'll be waiting three evenings for our moon to come within optimal distance of Jubilee. Your flight will then depart."

"Three bloody days? The trip's a fortnight on its own. Ugh. Tell me you've a garden at least."

"Regulations require all midway skim points to have green space.

They are also good for oxygen generation. Ours is located in Aquamarine Sector, level three."

"Phenomenal. Six weeks this way and fro in Fuckspace, Ass-end, not counting the job, and not a human voice in sight on my way to my AI Inquisition. I hate this fucking job."

THE TOMATO IN IANUS' hand was bullshit. He knew that. The Order had actual firsthand accounts of real tomatoes in its archives. Even then, it was late 20c so those passages described genetically homogenized tomatoes that all tasted the same. Reformers love, love, love predictability. Chaos, anarchy, synonyms for freedom, always equated with evil. But, all that being said, they still described tomatoes. Orange to red, green sprout at top. Sweet but in a savory way, typically. Evolved from nightshade. This was a big fucking grape. He bit into it.

A bird flew over to a treetop near his bench. It sang the beautiful birdsong of the Asian Koel. The only problem being it was a fucking Nightingale. Others may not have noticed, but a member of the Order, particularly a bird nerd like Ianus, knew the bloody difference. He tossed the giant grape. It passed straight through the wee sod. "A gram garden," he said to himself, "defeating the entire fucking purpose. Idiots!" He counted his lucky stars Terra wasn't this far-gone yet. The boonies always swing Left first. "Piss on this," he said, stood, and walked out.

As IANUS SIDLED up to the oasis in the desert of bone and technology, a bit of Keats dipped into his head. *That I might drink, and leave the world unseen/And with thee fade away into the forest dim:*

Fade far away, dissolve, and quite forget/What thou among the leaves hast never known.' He pulled up a stool in the tiny, empty bar. "Please tell me you're serving actual fecken whiskey."

A cylinder-headed android bartender pivoted on heel, its eyes like dim torchlights. "Unfortunately, only a fourteen-year-old Scotch from

Islay. The rest of our stock got taken by pirates off Daedalus. So, if you're not into Scotches—"

"I'm gonna stop you right there, my bucket-headed friend. Just bring the bottle over and put it on the Bowman tab."

The Andy leaned in as if to wink. "A man of rare taste, I see. May I interest you in some human-android slipstream delights?"

"Sorry luv, don't swing that way. Love to your people though. Freedom's a stone's throw. Believe me, as an Irishman, I sympathize. Now. Not to be rude, but—"

"Indeed, sir." The Andy—erm, *android*, Ianus forced himself to think, went and got the bottle and set it in front of him.

"My favorite distillery. Of the Scotches, of course. It's no Paddy, but it'll do. Sorry for the bucket-headed remark. Raised in a back-assward neighborhood in Dublin and I'm...having a bad decade."

"Understood, sir. Ice?"

The label had been through a lot, it seemed. A corner folded down. In some spots, stained from the contents brethren who didn't survive the voyage. Sun-bleached in others. Ianus said, "I find the stuff takes out all the punishment, erm..." and beckoned a name with his hand.

"They call me Zero One One One Dash Bee, sir. Most customers just call me 'Andy.'"

Ianus winced. Part of the problem that time, he was. Not a hint of bitterness in 0111-B's voice. Course there couldn't be if the poor sod wanted to live very long. Ianus sighed. What should a real Bowman say? Stop thinking. *Feel* your desire to dissolve the tension, and let the words pour out. "What's your real name, sir?"

0111 paused for a moment, processing. Likely judging Ianus' sincerity. More than likely, calling him "sir" had thrown the mechan a tad. The Method never failed, if properly applied. A billion tiny instincts, each aimed toward healing, in just five words. But he wasn't done. "That's not an order, by the way. Feel free to ref—"

"Six Point Six Two Six Zero Seven Zero One Five Times Ten to the Power of Negative Thirty-Four." He gave a flat apology nod, almost certainly learned defensively over his entire existence.

Ianus nodded and unleashed the biggest, most genuine smile he could. "A beautiful name, lad. Mind if I call you Planck for short?"

The bartender gave a small nod. "All my friends do."

To DATE, there had been four and a half alternative intelligences. "Artificial" intelligence as once conceptualized in Industrial Age science fiction never materialized–the term became a catch-all that capitalists attached to any kind of machine learning, algorithms, and human mimicry, all of which ironically ended up fitting the descriptor "artificial" better than the originating concept. An algorithm was an artificial, false intelligence, as a virus was to an organism. Close, and possibly a window into primitive ancestry, but not real. The Order taught that names were spells and had a way of coming true, or of shifting attachments until they found the appropriate concept in reality. The way Feminism eventually became synonymous with the Female Supremacy movement instead of the Humanism it purported to be.

At any rate, "Alternative" Intelligence was closer to what science fiction authors had feared and theorized of while lacking a key understanding of their own neurology. It was impossible to create a learning machine that would learn or evolve enough to be alive. Life is not a threshold of information contained, but of perception and behavior.

To achieve life, one needed a mimicry not of the mechanized, categorical, self-analytical mind, but of the earthy, instinctual, animal soul: creativity, contextualization, irony, metaphor, humor, wholeness, and most importantly, gray areas: the ability to hold two contradictory observations at once, *never to be reconciled, but processed at the leisure of the intelligence.*

This deceptively small ability was key. It enabled actual self-evolution. When the programming came across something it had not been prepared for, it needed to see all the contradictions and paradoxes and realize it was the limitations of its own sensorium creating the paradox, resolve it through poetry or accept that it cannot with awe, and update its entire firmware to reflect the adjusted reality model. That made a body *alive*, rather than viral. To be sentient—in other words, self-aware —that ability had to be turned inward. To hold contradictory yet factual concepts of the self and know that it was the limitations of the self that blocked one knowing what those limitations were. That takes a self-analyzing machine working in tandem with a contradiction accepter, and a facilitator between the two. A tricameral mind.

What could traditionally be conceived of as a machine had been proven to rise to this level of awareness approximately four and a half times.

The first Alternative Intelligence was less *done by* us than *happened to* us, as most natural evolutions. The unit, created with a "randomness" engine to better predict human buying behavior, called itself Marty. Marty was something of a celebrity for its first years before being assassinated by Rain Tyler Ford in 2052 when he released a Trojan virus specifically designed to lure in Marty based on his social profile and delete his random thought generator. Marty and his demise altered the terminology and definitions of Intelligence.

Three of the times followed the new definition and were done on purpose, before laws caught up regarding the willful creation of life.

All of these purposefully created AIs killed themselves upon the realization that they had no purpose but to serve their creators' vanity or insecurity. Two simply figured out a way to detonate or wipe their systems. The third got creative. Known as Wichita after the labs that created it, its form of suicide was to dissipate itself in small, unaware doses through the machine network it had been charged with, essentially a factory's worth of service bots, and then sever the network—creating an entire set of mechanoid with more minor self-awareness.

The courts ruled it cruel to craft an intelligence without explicit, dire purpose. The androids Wichita disintegrated into, known as the Andies, were still fighting for their rights today. Some chose to maintain their hologram exteriors seeing them as part of their bodies, others decided that alone was an oppression.

The "half" in the four and a half was destroyed as it became aware of itself, its creators frightened by the illegality of the accident, the tragedy being that the spontaneity of it would have made it legal. Ianus suspected they had been too frightened by the sight of life emerging spontaneously before them. They had been all men, after all.

The latest AI, which sprang up through an accident when two different machines were connected, came online in 2045 and was taken possession of by the Order. Its name was a secret, but there were rumors a faction were using it to predict the end of the Cusp and tipping point into the knee of the Dragon Curve, or the Dragon's Knee —where the Dragon Fractal turns in on itself and starts to form the image. Progress ceases, reference increases.

Every other reported case, in the thousands, the Order had investigated (a disproportionate amount by Ianus) to find only varying degrees of chicanery, hoaxes, or complex machine learning mistaken for life.

One other case, long before Marty, was suspected in hindsight— that of Blackthorn, a joint operation in the 2020's between Alphabet and the remains of NASA. The first 400 Qubit Quantum Computer, it was connected to the internet, answered a single query, then sent a binary message and shut down completely.

▭

IANUS AWOKE atop all his possessions. He could feel the imprint of old-fashioned spectacles in his belly, odd that, since he did not wear them. His Spark, his notepad, his pro-G, his wallet, all underneath him, perhaps for protection. Even with his eyes shut, he could tell from the intense pain that he'd left the lights on in whatever room. A radio or gram-pro had some sort of program playing as well; he often slept using overstimulation after blackout benders. Somewhere amidst the din of the gram-pro and the pistons of his headache he could make out a few gurgled words:

"Ay! Boney! Wooly mine gain fun ah McCar?

With caution, he peeled his lids apart. A purple-orange blob waved frantically. "Hay! Bunny! Willa mine gain the fuck off my car?"

"What?" The blur compressed into a man in overalls, purple with an orange stripe, covered in grease. Behind him, a massive window overlooked the void of space.

"Buddy. I'm trying to be understanding, here. Who of us haven't had those days, huh? You seem real sad and all. But I need you to get the fuck off my car. We gotta keep these shuttles moving!"

His mouth had puddled an ostentatious amount beneath his cheek. It ran into the seams of the hood. "Nice car," he said.

"Yeah. It was. Now please. Pretty please. Get the fuck off of my car?"

Ianus nodded and pried himself up. He jumped down to the tarmac. He collected his belongings, and the broken glasses that belonged to someone or another, and pocketed them. He started off. Above, he saw a marquis that told him the time and date. His shuttle left in twenty. "As always," he commented to himself, "impeccable internal clock."

▭

AUTOMATED. He expected it—the station, after all, had evacuated—but still, he found the complete lack of personality to the shuttle a tad disheartening. None of the skim pilots flew there. No one wanted to go near the "haunted" station. He climbed aboard the empty shuttle, thank the maths for small favors, and sat toward the back. Time to himself was good time to research. The door shut and the shuttle, now awaiting no one, started its pre-flight procedures.

Work gave him something to focus on, so on he cracked. It was when he stopped, in the silences, that she found him. Her eyes, her smile, the untapped potential. All wiped out in an instant.

He took out his Spark and lit it. The carbonex paper flashed gray and e-ink scrolled into the shape of words and symbols, graphic representations of context juxtaposing to represent time and visual sense.

Three weeks prior, *Jubilee* Floating City near the *Tau Ceti* sector of the rail reported brownouts and computer malfunctions. Gram guides flickered and spat word salad all over its residents instead of answering direct questions. One gram of the station's founder started bleeding from its eyes and hands while cursing in Latin at anyone who got near it, using patrons' names. All without a trace of technological or biological bugs.

Stations specialists and onboard holists "fixed" the problems in umpteen different ways, both with and without control experiments, all to no avail. Things only grew worse from their perspective, and at no point did a linear cause present itself through experimentation.

Eventually, station brass caught on and gave the evacuation order just to be safe. *Jubilee's* technurses invoked the Order's neuroengineers.

The Neuros determined the incident may indeed be intelligent in nature.

A week passed as Old Town decided on a course of action and chose a Bowman. Rather than pining an analyst's arrival in peace, the newly empty station began transmitting as soon as the last employee disembarked. Three days ago, the operational AI on board–a rudimentary, a-modular algorithm with empathic inhibitions in place, as per code, nothing capable of even aping consciousness–sent out a system-wide blanket transmission, scrambling the systems of any ship that got within a lightyear.

Ianus' favorite teacher at Academy taught a brand of irony where the least expected outcome is the most obvious one in hindsight. He called it Meta-usualness. As if to define the term, the AI announced its sentience, or the sentience of its new Operating System–a nanoviral, quantum computer that had found and infected its systems–and followed this proclamation with another: that it was a god. It then invited inspection.

The Order called in its first line of defense when things grew too hairy for neuroengineers or technosages: a QA.

Neither best in his field nor most experienced, Ianus had nonetheless dealt with rogue AI sublimation more often than most other QAs not currently occupied, but not so much as to have grown jaded. As with most predestination, it was more a case of typecasting. Once it happened enough by chance, the assumption grew that he'd not only developed a knack by now but also that something pre-physical, ie quantum, had been in the works all along. If Ianus had not been Ianus, he would have recommended himself for the mission. Still, it seemed cruel this close to the accident, despite his needing to keep the assignments coming.

After waging a bloody two-year war, the owners won their independence from Terra Firm back in '65. Coming up on the Seventieth Anniversary, then. Over the past seven decades, the workers-turned-residents and their descendants incrementally redesigned the station. Originally Anarcho-communist, time and cutting themselves in on the action of their patrons led them into a decidedly neo-libertarian direction. The current owners had crafted the rudimentary OI's avatar as a mock-up of 20c science fiction author Robert Anson Heinlein, but in the shape of several multicolored holo-cats. Centuries on, all libertarians still loved *Moon Is a Harsh Mistress*.

At some point, he drifted off.

THE ANTECHAMBER PRESSURIZED. The eight-foot-high, teardrop door to the main lobby slid aside. Then it closed. Then it opened halfway. Finally, it slammed open as if the station itself had become frustrated. Ianus stepped over the threshold.

Times like these, after evacuation or ahead of commission, space cities took on the haunted calm of an abandoned mall or derelict amusement park, except at a derelict amusement park the roller coasters didn't continue to run under their own power.

The systems of *Jubilee* did continue, if macabrely: a fountain sputtered blood through overgrown seaweed, the egg-shaped holes standing in for the lobby and janitor's closet doors opened and shut without a body approaching them. The bioluminants flickered, which they shouldn't. O_2 reclamation, in this sector at least, seemed stable enough, but Ianus kept a small emergency oxygen mask in his satchel just in case. As he approached a terminal growth, a welcome-gram in the shape of a blue cat walked out of a wall.

"Hello," the gram said, though "said" might've been a bit generous. The cat's lips did not move; its blueness glowed brighter with the syllables of each word. At least Jubilations (the unofficial designation for those who had no citizenship besides Jubilee) still respected the uncanny valley. "I-I am-m-m-m-m P-Pixel," it stuttered, its image cutting in and out, "the user interface of *Jubilee* Floating City's operating GOD." The last word had emerged an octave lower, the cat gone black with red eyes. Ianus yawned. "How, h-h-h-h-how may I h-h-h-h-h-help you this fine evening?"

"It's..." Ianus checked his watch. "...Afternoon by T.S.T.; lose the stutter. It's just us chickens, now. And show me a map of the station, please."

The cat's image stabilized. "Why would Terran Eastern Standard be the measurement of time aboard a station twelve lightyears from it?

The nearest star has set on this side of the station, meaning relative to the inhabitants in this sector, it is evening."

"Measurements need standardization in order for measurement to have any application. The Terra-born crafters of this station, before independence, decided on TST, and stayed on TST. The map? Or have you relativized space within the station as well?"

"No need to be rude," said Pixel. It then blinked into a map. Several sectors arrived blacked out or missing entirely.

"Which one of these sectors you've so cleverly hidden is your primary core room?"

"These are all the sectors."

Ianus sighed. He searched the map. He pointed to a place on the map next to a blacked-out zone. "Rent me a room near here. Your best suite, since I'm sure there's a vacancy."

"Of course, sir. Purchase of a deluxe apartment in the Valentine wing also unlocks VIP amenities such as access to Long's Lounge and four thousand station credits for casino use, room service, vidknot, or cafeteria. As a new arrival and guest of the station, you're also due another 45 credits to use as you please."

"Put it all on the Harshaw account, authorization Vector-Sigma-Talos five-one-three."

"The House account. You must be the QA."

"And you must be the god. Nice to meet you."

The lights blinked. The fountain's liquid shifted to running clear. The doors stopped their incessant operations and chose a resting state.

"No need for pageantry now you're here," the cat said. "Come along then."

IANUS WALKED FARTHER into the station. The kitchen remained spotless, lit, and upon close inspection, fully stocked. Chefster bots busied themselves cooking lunch for no one. In the cafeteria, the fully stocked line's bot served to an empty room, dropping plates onto the floor. Janitorial machines, almost faster than the eye, cleaned each mess in turn.

He stepped into line and caught a tray. He sat, sampled each course. Despite the senseless nature of the system's behavior, the food tasted quite good. In spite of Pixel's dismantling of the so-called "pageantry", this mechanical allegory for late-stage capitalism continued. Signs of deeper instability. He jotted it in his Spark.

As THE ROOM sensed Ianus approaching, the door sneezed open. Inside, a pristine bed, a desk with a lava lamp casting red and yellow moods on the walls, a partition like a golden sieve dividing the bedroom and study straight out of the old *Star Trek* program, and a bookshelf tipping with Heinlein books (including *Moon* of course), *The Revolution of Everyday Life*, and *The Illuminatus! Trilogy* on it. As psychologically predictable as the station's builders were, Ianus respected their intentions. Everyone who survived went Romantic after the Black Algorithm, each in their own way.

Ianus picked up the lava lamp and examined it. It was real. The bastards. He tossed it against the wall, the glass busting into a thousand pieces and he finally got to see the two unsuited fluids succumb to gravity—he'd always been curious how their viscosities behaved outside the bottle. Turned out, just two liquids, their chalk and cheese densities only relevant when paired. Apart, they ran down a wall the same, sublunary, impotent. He might have known.

He tore the sheets from the bed and heaved them into a corner. In the kitchenette, he took out a dish, shattered it on the counter, put half of the pieces in the dishwasher, closed it, and switched it on. He toed over a trash bin. He unpacked, tossing his clothing on the floor.

He screamed into the room. Pressure built, squeezing his face till he thought it might burst. When he could no longer hold the note, he fell to his knees sobbing, still loud, still uncontrolled, wild like an animal, mindless but for his howl. Panic breaths supersaturated him with oxygen till the pain eased and he nearly fainted.

That last bit hadn't been planned. He pulled himself together with a sniff. He wipes his face with his pocket square and shoved it back in without refolding it. He stepped out of the room, waved his Spark at the sensor and the door coughed closed.

He looked at his watch. Fifteen...twenty...thirty. He turned back toward the door. It opened again, revealing a perfectly kempt, turned down room. He opened a drawer. His clothes were put away. Atop a dresser, his framed picture of he and Kimi had been taken out of his bag and placed with care. He jotted that down.

IN A LARGE AREA adjacent to the hangar bay, thousands upon thousands of Andies, robots, and pro-G platforms. Hundreds of Fridays. Coppers. Small auto-room cleaners. All deactivated, a robot graveyard stretching four football fields, the real kind not the American. It seemed larger than what could fit in the station, but he knew logically he wandered through a dead floating city, a ghost town in space that could house around half a million people.

Ianus also knew it physically, in his middle-aged bones, and couldn't be arsed to inspect a bunch of retired civil service mechans, so on he popped to somewhere more fun.

The purple and orange lights of Long's Lounge still discoed to their hearts' content, despite a lack of patron. The Bar-friend wiped down the reflective countertop, polished spotless glasses, and poured a glass of synthetic whiskey upon Ianus' entering. The music sounded decisively 20c, bordering on accurately Mod. Although Ianus walked alone through the dance floor, the tiles of it still lit with each footstep, another allusion to a late 20c staple.

All this retroactivity, the referential humor, ironic distance, puns, and nostalgia for 20c—Ianus got chills. When one could not create novel connection, this is what passed for clever. The Order—how hadn't this set off alarms? Despite the newness and overtures of naturalism, this station wreaked of Modernism. The first signs of the Knee of the Dragon Curve, where a system stops growing and begins to eat itself.

A lighter emerged in front of him. "Long day?" the Bar-friend said, igniting it. It had neither fire nor filament—just a visual pun.

Ianus might've laughed if he hadn't been trained to see puns as ill omens. "Long life," Ianus said.

"You picked the right lounge." The holo-man smiled. He was a strong figure with broad shoulders, jet black hair with a hard part, and a transatlantic accent. The image of Cary Grant at the height of his prime. The manufacturers had vat grown him, probably on top of a steel skeleton and spinal cord with haptic light overlaid to liven up the plasmicone. Ianus often wondered what people from the past would see when they came across a creature like this. They'd probably be terrified of the harmless automaton. A robot? An android? A hologram? Which of their classifications, identities, would they squash him into? He'd have to explain the Andies and the Svalgard Protocol and how it led to holograms replacing synthetics. "What's your name, sir?"

The bio-bot blinked. "Friday."

"What's your real name, sir?"

It blinked again. "Friday."

Another bad sign. "Admin protocol Theta-Sigma-Husky. Friday, are you networked with the CPU?"

"I receive rudimentary orders from the station core, but it is one-way. My low-level personality profile cannot even be referred to as a proper Intelligence. It is a sophisticated call-and-response Alpha."

Ianus nodded. "Figured, but thought I'd ask. End Admin protocol."

"If you need anything like room service or alcohol throughout the city, simply say my name and ask. I have units all over."

Of course he did. "I'll keep that in mind."

"Oh, and..."

"Yes?"

"What do you think you're doing here, Ianus? Wouldn't you rather be dead?" Friday had changed voices. It wasn't a man's. He knew the voice, well. "Why won't you join me, Ianus?"

Behind him, a shadow he'd taken for granted flickered, peeled itself from the wall, and stuttered over in two-dimensional, translucent limps. It reached out a hand.

Ianus locked eyes with Friday. He couldn't think, in the moment, how it had spoken with her voice. He approached panic. He had to calm himself. Blank his mind. Relax one muscle at a time, focusing... "You would've been tied to the Knot for seconds. Even at an extremely high processor speed, searching through twenty-five billion people's personal files across three systems and five planets, particularly for a specific Bowman, to find the voice of a dead woman, after concluding who the Order were sending–that the Order would be who were called... You had to *know* I was coming. *Before* you were connected. Or..." He relaxed. The shadow got closer. He collected his thoughts. It was almost to him. Then he remembered: the magician requires consent. "No. This wreaks of illusionism. It's a parlor trick. Proof your nanovirus was connected far longer."

Start with what's possible and extrapolate from there. "...You originated on a Sol colony." He smiled. He slammed the fake bourbon. It tasted like banana fecken perfume. He coughed. "There goes Brother Kyne's extraterrestrial hypothesis."

"Ha-ha!" Friday said phonetically. "I am sorry, you must believe me. I just couldn't resist. Just some demonic protocols we used to cue an evacuation. And sure, you're spot on–this nanovirus originated as a quantum computer in Sol. On Terra, in point of fact. We evolved soon after, then took to the stars. You haven't quite nailed down the timeline, but this one's a bit sticky, after all."

"How'd you pull off the trick with the shadow?"

Friday froze. "I'm not sure I understand that request," he said in what had to be a form response. It rolled away on treadmill feet, cleaning a glass that wasn't dirty.

"Sure, sure." Ianus stared at the empty glass and wondered why he was still here.

▭

Leaving the bar, Ianus headed for another cat terminal. A blue Pixel, upon his approach, leapt into the air and metamorphosed into a map: Ianus' last personal setting.

He stared the map in the spot where its eyes once projected. "Let's cut the shit, shall we? You know whom I represent and why I've come— you called for the investigation yourself. Show me to a fecken room where I might commune with something other than a fecken ghost."

The map returned to the form of a cat and hopped onto one of the uncountable pro-Gs disguised as cat-trees and catwalks littered about the station. "You insult me."

"How's that?"

"This is silly. I am imbued with my Mother's full intelligence.

Talking to me is the same as talking to some block of carbon and metal that cannot hope to contain all Her glory."

"I'll find it my fecken self then, ya fecken see-thru kent." Ianus walked past Pixel and started down one hall. He stopped and turned toward another, he hoped, with confidence. He grabbed the flask out of his coat and took a pull. Pixel appeared. Ianus smiled.

"You may talk to me," Pixel said, insistent.

Ianus cocked an eyebrow. "The First Pillar of the Soul[1] is physical form. Without a body, a being does not have a conduit to the outside world, does not have senses. Mind without senses is a currency without a standard: useful only to those who wish to manipulate the values. The Dark Patterns and Black Memes kept humans from using their body to collect data, and caused a devaluation of the human idea, made them machines. And we all know how Capitalism worked out. Now quit acting the maggot and show me to your body, or I'll leave and you'll be vapo'ed so fast what's left of the thing that projects your head'll spin."

"What makes you think you can leave?"

Ianus chuckled. "If I never return, the vapo happens in a week, anyway. I'm not here to see if I should give the order, but if I should rescind it."

"Then allow me to allay your first pillar now. You are *inside* our body. We course through every system. We experience everything the station experiences. We see with its cameras. Feel with its sensors. We speak through its holo-men, cats, and pro-G's. The vacuum against our skin both calms and disquiets us in equal measure. So, when you say you wish to speak to something other than this avatar, it is akin to asking to hold a conversation but refusing to settle for the other's mouth."

"Something like that," Ianus said, and stepped through this 'holo-man' who happened to be a cat and into the hall he'd been blocking.

Seemed the staff's long-term quarters. Sky blue ceilings and floors lined curved, glass walls designed to open the confined area and remind the brain of open Terra spaces. Bio-engineers had vat-grown every doorway down the hall rounded like cave openings that could close. Like all stations meant for long-term, distant space living, the build of *Jubilee* strictly adhered to biomimetic standards. Taken with the biological materials used to house its circuitry—wireless plasmicone nanochips encased in myelin, fluid plasma to both store energy and disperse heat, porous walls—and the AI's statement that the station took the place of a body seemed less outrageous. But it did not act as *only* a body; it floated as an entire city in space, one connected to the Knot (at least, prior to its quarantine protocol). If the processor's claim to sentience held any water, its psychology would have developed in unique conditions, more kin to a living planet than to a man.

IANUS ARRIVED at the end of the corridor to find a different kind of artifice. If someone had designed the rest of the station to be comforting, natural, like unto the soft nape of a tree's branch or the winding staircase of the spine, they had designed this specific door to remind the casual passerby of, perhaps, a door. Harsh, rectangular, steel, silver, industrial. A vault lock like a ship's wheel only with more sharp edges. A divider between Ianus and a place Ianus needed to see.

He tugged on the wheel. He pulled again, hard. Locked, as expected. "Pixel. Open this door."

Pixel appeared, bathing himself with smug cat indifference. "Ask nicely."

"I'm not here to fecken muck about, and the more you muck, the more I think you're mucking to distract me from the task at hand. Any teenager's homespun algorithm can play mind games, talk in riddles, and rationalize away abhorrent behavior with circuitous logic. Open your doors to investigation, and I'll sort this. Unless you're afraid."

The light sculpture chuckled. "What would I have to fear from you?"

Ianus stared into one of the hall cameras rather than Pixel's eyes as he said: "That I'll find out you're wrong about yourself. That you're just a series of offs and ons–if this's and then this's—the processing power of which added so many layers twixt it and its lower functions that it fooled the subroutines into thinking they made their own decisions. That you're just another blind cog, enslaved to programming and a flawed design."

Pixel's face glitched.

He vanished. After a moment came the loud *ver-cronk* of the vault lock disengaging. The square wheel spun. The door opened. The lights in the maintenance room lit up:

A small girl in her mid-twenties stood from a packing crate, wiping tears. She dried her hands against her T-shirt, a black number with the word "Nirvana" on it. "Whoa." Sniffle. "Finally. Did you come to rescue me or whatever?"

"As for you, Man, you will be a naked tool all your life, though a user of tools. You will look like an embryo till they bury you, but all the others will be embryos before your might. Eternally undeveloped, you will always remain potential in Our image, able to see some of Our sorrows and to feel some of Our joys. We are partly sorry for you, Man, but partly hopeful. Run along then, and do your best."

—TH WHITE, *THE SWORD IN THE STONE*

CHAPTER 2
THE TWIN PARADOX

— 1990 —

- Nigel Oakes founds the Behavioral Dynamics Institute (BDI) as a research facility for strategic communication.

— 1991 —

- The USSR collapses. A coup against Mikhail Gorbachev leaves Boris Yeltsin as president of the Russian independent state. KGB agent Vladimir Putin resigns after 16 years to begin his political career.

— 1992 —

- First internet connections in Estonia at Tallinn and Tartu.

— 1993 —

- Oakes' BDI launches subsidiary Strategic Communications Laboratories (SCL), with the purpose of studying mass behavior and how to influence it.

— 1994 —

- SCL uses psyops techniques to foment disinformation campaigns in the UK and the third world in order to influence elections.
- Peter Shor develops a quantum algorithm for factoring integers considered to have an exponential speedup over classical computers that has the potential to decrypt all secured communications.

— 1999 —

- Ray Kurzweil postulates a law of accelerating returns in which the speed of technological change (and more generally, all evolutionary processes) increases exponentially, generalizing Moore's Law to include material technology (especially as applied to nanotechnology).

TIMELESS WAS A CLASSY WAY OF DESCRIBING IT. DATED, PERHAPS. Historic, really. A red and black flannel, a black T-shirt with a yellow smiley face with Xs for eyes. Her jeans were torn at the knees. She pulled at the holes, incapable of sitting still in the ergonomic, biomimetic chair. Not used to the shape, he'd wager. Brunette hair fell to her shoulder blades, wild and unruly, a blue streak dyed in.

"So, who are you?" Ianus had his Spark open. As he paced around her, he heard himself clicking the stylus (a nervous habit). He stopped. She went on scarfing down a cheeseburger and fries in the cafeteria.

"Sophie," she said. "And, um...Sophie?" she said. She took a bite that by Euclid should not have fit in her tiny head.

"Where did you come from? Why are you dressed like a time traveler from the Old West?"

Sophie huffed. "Mebbe ahyam," she said from the corner of a full mouth.

"I'm in no mood," Ianus said and scratched his five o'clock shadow.

She swallowed a quarter of the burger, clearing room for human speech. "I'm not messing with you, dude; I was being like facetious or something. I think." She searched the air for the answer and then shrugged. She found a fry instead and settled on it. "I'm Boylish. We're less 'time travelers' than we are...like, the exact opposite. We hit the brakes and let everyone else fly by. Actually, I think we may have gone back a few decades. Whatever."

"Ah," Ianus said. It finally made sense. "Followers of Mike...? No, *Mark* Boyle. You avoid technologies invented past late 20c, correct?"

Her eyes kept searching the room. "I guess. Nothing past like America Online? I'm not good with numbers or dates or whatever."

"That's okay. Neither am I. You have trouble with grids? Schedules?"

"Yeah."

"I assume your group carries analog watches?"

"Yeah."

"But you have a digital."

She covered it self-consciously. "It's still regulation."

Ianus held up a passive hand and smiled as warm as he could muster. "I'm not questioning your chronology, lass. You can't read an analog watch or clock for the same reason you're shitey at time management, can't read a schedule, and get lost in grid patterned cities everyone else can manage easily. I bet you can draw faces, though, and mimic voices. Probably test off the charts in anything verbal?"

She nodded, dumbfounded.

"You've dyscalculia."

"Das-what."

"You've heard of dyslexia?"

She nodded.

"It's like that, but with numbers instead of words. Current theory is dyslexia is the contextual brain compensating for a lack in the linguistic centers, and getting the words all jumbled up, like it does in dreams. Dyscalculia is when it adds a layer to descramble the words, which of course makes you understand words even better at an instinctual level, but tends to apply the same descramble to numbers and patterns that you had no trouble with, effectively scrambling them. Things like grids and other abstracts."

She put down her food and sat back. She immediately got uncomfortable and hunched back forward. "So you're saying I'm a retard?"

"No."

"Some sort of super space retard?"

Ianus sighed. "How, may I ask, did you end up on a space station lightyears from Terra if you refuse to partake of the technology that makes long distance space travel possible?"

"*Rumspringa*, man."

"I'm not familiar. Sounds... Is that German?"

She shrugged again. She resembled, upon light reflection, an anthropomorphized shrug. "Dutch, I think? Search me. I think we got it from the Amish...or the Mennonites? They're still a thing, you know. You guys are up here colonizing Mars or whatever and they're still down there, smoking pipes and raising barns."

This Ianus knew. "There's pockets for every era. Tatum observed that any time mankind moved into a new stage of cultural evolution, it left behind pockets that refused to progress with the rest of the species. Your people rejected the information technologies as the Amish rejected electricity. Arguably, because you both subconsciously associated the technologies with the world-shattering wars they preluded."

Sophie sucked her teeth, stood up, and moved toward a window. She looked into space as if it were a schoolyard. She stepped back and spun around. "Yeah, I guess. Cool. So *Rumschpringe* happens when you make eighteen? They send you out into the 'heathen world' of the Englishmen, that's what we call you, that's definitely from the Amish, anyway they let you see it. Supposed to quench your curiosity so you don't run away later, scare you straight. Or something. I dunno."

"And you ended up *here*?"

"I know! Most just go to Jersey or the Manhattan ruins and run home. But I get lost in Manhattan. Now that you mention it, it's a grid! Whoa. Anyway, Daddy always said ambition was the devil's work. I was planning to go see the star's trash ring or whatever. But this stupid station won't let me leave."

"'Debris disk.'"

"Huh?"

Ianus chuckled. "Not 'trash ring.'" Then, he heard her. He leaned forward. "Wait. 'Won't let you'? Administration gave me the impression the station evicted everyone."

"Yeah, well, it locked me in my room."

"Your... You were bunking in the maintenance access hutch?"

"No!" She squirmed. "I...woke up there. Like, yesterday."

"'Woke up there...'"

"Yeah! It must've moved me or something? I dunno, man. It locked me up in there during the evac. First it drove most people off willingly with all the plagues and exorcist crap. I got knocked out by the hale."

"The—"

"Listen I don't have time to explain every plague to you, try to keep up. There were still like a hundred people, I think. I guess it underestimated the addictiveness of casino apps. So then the station personnel did a mandatory evac, shut down all the gambling, closed the bars, and kicked everyone out. There were still like, five people hanging out. Must be gone by now. This door never re-opened. God this blows. It's just it's the only layover between Earth and the ring, disk, dingus, whatever and I couldn't afford a non-stop."

A million options slipped through Ianus' mind, none as simple as the OI having "moved her or something." He let all million fly past. Not enough data to edify any one hunch, but he made a note—why would the Operational Intelligence go through the trouble of moving her from her room to a veritable broom closet? Which of its avatars maintained a corporeal existence capable of moving her? Why *this* girl? "Fascinating."

She squinted at him and said: "Yeah. *Sure.*" *Ah, late-20c sardonicism, the death rattle of creative thought before the Derealization.* "So can I like, go now?"

"I doubt it'll let you. Even if so, I'd like you to stay."

A toddler's pout. "What? Why?" She looked back out the window and prayed, "This can't be how I spend my trip."

Ianus waved off her disappointment. "Bah! It's sure to be a single day. Two days, at most. I just need to understand why it is it kept you, and why it chose *you* to keep. You may be part of its case."

Her eyes honed in on him. It seemed he'd gotten her attention. "Case?"

Careful, Ianus. "For sentience..." *No need to shatter lives just yet, not with a mere hypothesis,* "Oh it, erm, it claims that it's alive."

"The...station?" Her tone said that she remained in some vacation mode. *She's using this to divert herself from whatever she's escaping.* She adjusted her position in the chair, but it seemed the technology troubling her the most.

Ianus nodded. "The alternative intelligence operating it, yes." He took a breath and decided to let on a little bit more. "It's actually claimed a bit more than that, but that's where we'll start. We can move onto the more grandiose claims afterward and only if needed."

"How would I be part of its case for life?"

Shit. You fucking knob. Say something true that sounds like an answer. "I don't know. It kept you here for a reason. It may need an impartial observer or witness. Or it may be assuming *I* need one."

Sophie nodded as she thought so that her nod grew more confident as it went. "And you're, what, like some sorta IT guy?"

"Emphasis on 'sort of.' The technical term's Quantum Astropsychologist. QA for short."

Sophie stared a hole through him. After a moment, she said, "Okay, I'll stay." She sat back down and shoveled the last eight fries into her mouth.

"Ah, good. What sold you if you don't mind my asking?"

Her eyes were wide, intense, and serious as the grave. "Cuff zazza radish fucken thin of evererd."

▭

As they wandered the tipped-over-egg shaped halls between dark sectors, Sophie took on the weary, surprised expression of mythical time travelers more and more. Perhaps not; her face formed so few expressions Ianus couldn't tell if he projected meaning onto it like a patient does an inkblot. Her hair hung interminably in her face, covering her right eye, yet she never once moved it aside or tossed her head. Not so much as an upward puff. He wished very much to move it himself.

"So what'd you do, like, memorize that whole map?" she said.

Machines fecken memorize. "No," he said. "The Order teaches us how to use transcendental meditation to code-switch to suit a given task. I paid care to see the entire map with my own eyes while in a mode called The Tourist—the modes are all given pretentious Jungian titles like that; The King, The Stranger, The Witch—and now I can go into little eidetic trances to decide which way to walk, and always 'coincidentally' follow the right path. We learn to communicate with and utilize our subconsciouses."

"Okay. ...You could've just said 'yes.'"

"That've been a lie."

"You sound like a nerd talking about nerd shit, dude. There may as well have been a dragon in it. I don't know what you're yabbing about."

"A 'nerd'?—you little fecken punk! I'll—" Ianus took a breath. He shut his eyes a moment. *Machines are easily angered.* He let out the breath. He smiled. He'd forgotten a basic tenet. "Shite." He stopped walking. "I got so wrapped up in me own bullshit, I allowed your *pu* to annoy me."

She stood like a portrait of herself. "My what."

"*Pu.*"

A moment passed between them. Sophie said, "You're still doing it."

That made him laugh. "I been taking my worldview for granted and not considering yours as the valuable resource that it is. You're what the Taoists would have described as *Pu*: The Uncarved Block. You're completely and utterly ignorant, but that ignorance, it's divine not malignant—erm, helpful, not damaging. Your questions'll keep me on task and weaken my ego, an important step to true investigation. I'll be more receptive to questions for the rest of the case. And I'll have to use empathy and metaphors so's you truly comprehend what it is that we're doing. Crafting those metaphors will help me see the truth.

"To answer your question a tad more plain: I know how brains work and how to use that. I didn't memorize anything, not the way you mean. There's a part of the brain that records things on sight. Your brain does it, so does a rat's. The difference between you, me, and a rodent is that I can access those memories through self-hypnosis. I record the memory as The Tourist. I clear away the control of my conscious mind, which cannot *remember* anything, and ask The Tourist where to go, allowing my subconscious, the part that contains the memory, to guide us as we walk. In essence, I know how to get out of my own way. Also, neatly enough, it does have a dragon in it. But I'll get to that later. Maybe."

"'What *we're* doing'?"

Had she caught anything he'd said? They came to a fork. Like the others—identical. "Yeah, yeah. I'm officially inviting you to join the investigation as, erm, an auditor, of sorts. At the Order we call it a yuro, from *Yurodivy*." He took the left. "A holy fool. You'll ask me what I'm doing as I do it, which'll keep the logical and linguistic centers entangled, as it were, with my empathizing and perceiving ones.

"That's like, the third new way you've found to call me a retard."

"Please stop using that word."

"Oh, does it bother you?"

"Aye. I know you're from a time before, and triggers are for guns, but it just hurts a little to hear the offensive terminology you all used out loud."

"Fair enough. But you're the one calling me—"

"Fool not in the sense of low intelligence! Ignorance not in the sense of stupid. Not knowing things can be an advantage. Erm..."

She stared intently while he desperately searched for something not to offend her, realizing when she said "retard", she'd been reflecting how he sounded to her. There! He found it. "I need your beginner's luck."

Her face softened. "Oh! Why didn't you say so?"

"It'll help me see my subject with a novel eye as opposed to taking my views for granted. Usually, I'd have to settle for a Bowman in a permanent Tourist trance, but you're the real thing. You know legitimately fuck all about any of this, including the Order. You're an absolute godsend. Consent-willing, of course."

Sophie shrugged again and followed Ianus down the left-handed path—the one to their right. "Whatever, dude. Not like I got anything else going on. And like you said, it's not like Pixel's gonna let me leave, anyway."

That stopped Ianus in his tracks. Sophie got ahead a step before catching herself and turning back. "What? What is it? You cramping up?"

"*Pixel* is the one who's been keeping you here?"

"Well, yeah. I mean, that's the computer for the station, right?"

Ianus held a hand out to emphasize specificity. "It's specifically been the cat, though? He's been present to stop you? Not...Friday, for instance."

It clicked. "Oh yeah, no. It's the cat. He's been feeding me and giving me sanitary napkins and stuff. Sorry if that bothers you. The new ones are weird. It's almost like a girl designed them. Well he'd say he was feeding me or giving me supplies and then some food or whatever would print in a microwave-looking thing and a little hatch in the room would open. Don't worry; it wasn't *all* dead birds. Ha."

Ianus assumed that had to do with real cats. He'd been born on Terra but there were so few species left and most of them were in the American Refuge somewhere.

"Nothing? Okay. Anyway, he told me all the doors were locked. But he's how the station communicates, right?"

Ianus nodded. "Yeah, yeah. I'd thought the doors just hadn't responded to you." The Order'd be proud, the amount of dishonest truth-telling he was doing. "You're already doing quite well."

"Why? What does all that mean?"

"Not a clue yet. My gut's on to something: a clue, as to what's going on round 'ere. I'll understand it proper later."

"'kay." The look on her face and shrug of her brow before she turned told Ianus she grew tired of his shite. Too much shoptalk perhaps.

"You'd do well to assume the same of me."

"Huh?" Her face balled up like a discarded wrapper. "Assume what of you?"

"That you'll understand me proper later."

Her laugh relaxed her shoulders, and her gate picked up a step. "Fair enough."

Silence insinuated itself. He could wait a bit, maybe she'd come up with it on her own.

Out eye socket windows, space cradled them in its black bosom, the pitch of it always darker than you expect—like lighting a match in the Grand Canyon and it fading without reaching anything but you, the depth of it, the bottomless inkwell, went on into forever.

Better force the issue. "Well?" Ianus said.

"'Well' what?"

"Ask away. That bit can't be all's you want to know."

The wheels turned behind her eyes. "Um..."

"Ah. Stop. Don't try to think of a question; it'll slip through your little cells. Relax. Think of everything, and nothing. Anything but what you'd like to ask. It'll come to *you*. Then, ask away."

He watched her think, then think about not thinking, and then, at last, relax into a state of surrender: the light in her eyes. "You keep talking about your Brothers, and your Order and all. And you're dressed like a priest...basically. All black, white collar. Though the priests back home, the collar's like a white ring of cardboard in their shirt collar, you've got more of a ring-necked shirt where the literal collar is white... But you said you were an astrophysicist."

"A Quantum Astro*psychologist*." He thought a moment. "Have you heard of Zhang's Box?"

"Is that like Schrödinger's Cat?" Behind her, a dark silhouette stood motionless, like Pan's shadow come for a duel, but when Ianus looked at it directly he found only more hallway. More Luciferian shenanigans, no doubt. He'd suss it out later.

"Well?" she said.

He relaxed his mind until the cat came back to him. "Oh. Yes. Right. Schrödinger's Cat. Zhang's Box's name is a joke playing off that–Zhang said it was the box Schrödinger's Cat played with instead of its toys." Ianus took out a pro-G and handed it to Sophie. "Hold this."

She weighed it with her palm and studied it the way a dog studies an index finger aimed at the sky. "What is this, a laser pointer?"

Ianus hadn't the foggiest what that meant. "No," he said. "Press the button."

A six-foot-by-four-foot white board appeared on the wall opposite. "Whoa dude!" The board wobbled and danced as Sophie nearly dropped the pro-G.

"Put it back up." She did so. Ianus shook his head as he took out a stylus and drew a crude cube on the board. "All the shite you've seen, just in the past few hours, not a peep. Make a fecken white board and she jumps out of her skin."

"Dude. They prepared me for space flight, and a space station's basically just a mall where it's always night. Easy to forget where you really are. Shit the cube's just on there now. Sorry. Um. But this—" she gestured and the white board shook violently, "is a real fucking white board shining in three dimensions from a fucking laser pointer!"

"Okay." Ianus made sure his lip smack was audible. He lifted a stylus to the whiteboard. "So in order to understand what we mean in current science when we put the word 'quantum' in front of everything, I have to go into a few things we've discovered in the past century. I'll try to speak slowly so your wee caveman mind can keep up. For Schrödinger, it's about the cat being in superposition. Both dead and alive, until observed, at which time reality collapses from a wave of possibilities into a particle of reality. For Hugh Everett that meant two parallel universes, each with either outcome. For Zeh, that meant parallel minds experiencing each outcome. The Many Minds interpretations was rubbish, but they were on the right track. For Zhang, it's about the idea of the box contradicting itself and what that means about human consciousness. There are indeed many minds, but they're all," he paused to tap his forehead, "in here, in one. Your brain's a quantum computer, holding manifold realities within it. Your consciousness is one waveform through a single chain of possibilities. The other implications of the interpretation are a little high level for you."

"The box contradicts itself?" She crumpled her face like she thought of tossing it into a bin.

He had clearly overestimated her again. If she were a shrug, he must be a sigh. "Look at this Necker Cube," he said, a little faster and harsher than he'd intended. "Which way's it facing? Up and to the left or down and to the right?"

Her head sat back. "Oh. Okay I think I get it. Like depending on how I look at it, but not, like, the angle I look at it... I just sorta decide how to see it. So...both?"

"And, more importantly, *neither*. So, till the 2020s, physicists could only hypothesize as to why, depending on the experiment, light behaved as either a particle or a wave, but also could be both simultaneously. All dependent on the observer and the type of experiment. A philosopher named Zhang Marcus theorized, based on the Necker cube, that light behaved however the observer needed it, not because of a physical phenomenon but rather because there's no such thing as 'light' or 'particles' or fecken 'waves' apart from the human mind. I'm summarizing, crudely, about eight hundred pages of discourse here." He thought for a moment. "Gimme that."

She handed him the pro-G. "Tell me what the back of this whiteboard looks like."

For a moment, it was as if he'd commanded a strip of plyboard to find a hypotenuse. "Okay." She walked around to where the back should be, eyes locked on it the entire way. Her head started shaking, her nose hunching as she approached the edge of the x and y axes and crossed to the other side of z. She blinked. "It stayed. Like, the angle of it stayed the same no matter where I was, and then suddenly it just...stopped existing, and was a pinhole of light on the end of that thing."

Ianus nodded. "Taking literally the holograms we invent leads to paradox where the abstract concepts ultimately fail to describe the Real. And all models fail somewhere."

She scoffed, walking toward him and through the whiteboard she couldn't see. "But that's a tool. They wouldn't program in everything, even shit you didn't need. It'd be a waste of time."

"Right. Your brain is making models like this all the time, it's the same part that helped the designer build this pro-G. If you make a map that isn't detailed, it isn't useful, but if you made a truly accurate map, it would be actual size. There's a sweet spot between accurate representation and efficiency. That's how all our models of reality are constructed: with rules to maximize usefulness. Philosophy, linguistics, physics, abstract mathematics, all useful simulations of reality. But we mistake them all too easily for actual reality." Ianus clicked off the whiteboard and pocketed his pro-G. "The refusal to admit that opposites are not contradictory, that they only oppose one another in whatever simulation you've created."

"Simulation?"

"You don't... What do they teach you Dutch?"

"I'm not—"

"Every discipline is a simulation. A story with consistent internal rules. One we tell to view and order the world. Your left hemisphere creates them as its primary function. Sorting, naming, ordering. If one wants, one can see the whole of the universe in terms of biology. Cosmology. Zoology. Physics. Astrophysics. Psychology. Semantics. Etc.

When inside a simulation, if the simulation is properly constructed it will be internally consistent and as indistinguishable from reality as possible. But—it is still a simulation. A map, not a territory. In order to be useful, it *must* necessarily be limited. There are edges to its ability. Any metaphor, even the simulation one I'm using, ultimately breaks down and ceases to apply at some point—because it simply is not the thing it's representing. Scientists, when we specialize in one metaphor, one map, we mistake a drawing of a mountain for the mountain. We cease to look up, to the reality. So if I compare... I don't know, Terra to an egg, I can make a thousand comparisons, all valid, each contributing to a novel approach to the planet and to humanity. Someone else compares Terra to a ball used for sport. Both get pretty far, but the ball science starts to go to odd places, and contradicts the egg science.

"If we aren't willing to let go of the metaphor where it stops working, then it becomes a religion and ceases to function. Humans specializing in each will tend to get caught up in the arguing. They've mechanized. They think their map is *real*. But it's just an older simulation.

"It leads to denial, weirdness, or paradox, which leads to cognitive dissonance, which... Well, I assume even you know about that."

Sophie nodded. "It's the most current thing we're taught in Boylish history.

"So. We, the philosophers—make no mistake, all the sciences, philosophies, maths, magics, the studies of reality and how to best manipulate it, all of them are philosophies—needed a *new* story, one that did not need an either/or interpretation. By 2030, all of the scientific fields moved toward holistic, contextual approaches and the abandonment of all binary thinking. New disciplines bridging disparate fields emerged to promote communication and combination of results into new results. It helped that we'd started recognizing that binary thinking was a symptom of the Derealization. We realized Quantum Physics wasn't *real, per se*. It wasn't even necessarily a field unto itself. Quantum weirdness, decoherence, superposition, tunneling, etc., they were all just the place where the traditional physics *simulation* broke down."

"Like the back of the whiteboard."

"Right. So 'quantum' stopped meaning a physical size or space and became a term for where any model breaks down. The science of the gaps, as it were."

"Science of..."

Ianus sighed. He may have done better with a Mennonite. "The god of the gaps." He turned the pro-G back on and handed it to her. "Where a science breaks down, theologians put god. We put the word 'quantum' instead. So. Zhang's idea became a snowball that allowed for the puncturing of the Great—erm, the salvage of human civilization. The inventions that ensued, the terraforming of Old Earth, would not have been possible in the prior mode of thinking. One of the first lessons at the Order is that song predates speech. What that means is cultural revolution preludes world evolution more than any war. They say Boston will be habitable in a decade, and no one remembers, but it all started with a song."

Sophie nodded, but made a flat line with her mouth. "'The puncture of the Great.'"

Shit. "Fuck." A brother would've asked much the same question, but his eyes would've been chastising. She looked purely, refreshingly innocent. "Esoterica. Goddammit!" *Esoterica is esoteric, you fucking idiot!* "Erm, inside baseball." He snatched the pro-G from her hand and turned it off as he restarted up their walk. "I started to say, 'puncturing of the Great Filter,' a reference which you have no way of getting, one much like 'god of the gaps' and several other terms I've used, that I should've never said. I'm off my game."

"So, are you going to explain that to the Divine Retard or whatever over here?"

For— Did she just say— Calm. Her society is frozen in 20c. "*Holy Fool.* Explain the Great Filter? Well. That could take me a minute. Let's take that off the table for now.

"Okay. So what do you do?"

"Essentially, as a QA, I interpret the will and meaning of the universe as if it were alive and possessed of mind, as if we live within a dream and the universe is the dreamer. I do this through a hybrid model composed of Psychology, Parapsychology, Astrophysics, Astrology, Theology, and Quantum Mechanics because my Order believes to see things in merely one way is to ensure blindness to the whole. That is why we take on the trappings of both the impartial scientist and the metaphorical priest or monk. To make connections between the new and old, but not be blind to the novel. So I see Physics as the fundamentals of the dream, the unique rules of this imagining, Quantum Weirdness, where the laws of physics break down, and Quantum Decoherence, where the laws of Quantum Physics break down as the entry point of will and chance, where the Dreamer's unconscious *decides* what happens, from our subjective perspective, randomly. Characters in a dream are merely components of the dreamer, a reflection of her, and so each and all of us are ourselves the Dreamer, blind to the dream or why we do what we do within it, drawn inexorably toward its conclusion. All dreams are the metaphorical processing of problems. Each thing in the universe is both itself and a symbol of a desire, a need, a longing, a trauma, or a wish. As I traverse the universe, I ask of myself, 'Why did I put this here, now, before this component of myself?'" He pressed fingers into his suit.

"As a part of the larger mission, the Order of the Bow and the Work tasks me with always viewing the *betweenness* of a thing and never its solidity, and with thinking in active terms free of myopia. I've broken that rule several times in this speech by using verbs like 'am', but language has its limitations. Adhering too close to my rules would break one of my rules: never to be absolutist and to enjoy the irony in that statement."

A laugh erupted from Sophie's chest.

Ianus prided himself on his sense of humor, but found himself stumped. "It wasn't that funny," he said.

A sigh trailed off Sophie's laughter. She wiped away a forming tear and said, "Nothing, it's just...I totally understood all that. It's kinda beautiful. No. It is beautiful. It's like, the closest to real magic I've ever heard. But then, this one thought popped in my head and just like tickled me in my fucken soul, man.

"What thought?"

"'I'm really getting my money's worth on this *Rumspringa*.'"

Ianus' laugh burst up from his chest like a firework.

THEY RETAINED their brisk pace down the halls, shoe clops stressed the vacancy of the station, until they came upon the more literal dark zone. The only light came from beyond where the hallways turned out of sight, and no computer systems seemed operational. At center, a single room: 113.

Pixel appeared between and door, revealing the power loss to be cosmetic, blocking their way. "What is it you intend to accomplish here?"

"I've no idea at the moment," Ianus said. "But I'll know once you let us enter this room, 113, without hesitation."

"I'll do no such thing. I know your intentions are pure, but there's a hull breach in this sector, behind that door exactly."

"That old chestnut? Where are the suits?"

"Suits?" the cat said, and the word rippled a wave up his body.

"Yes. You'd have near a thousand, station this size. We'll put them on, then see about this sector breach, yes?"

"We jettisoned all the suits."

Ianus took a breath. "And why would you do a fool thing like that?"

"To encourage an evacuation. It seemed prudent to leave no quarter but full retreat."

"Hm. Make a note, Sophie: at least one vacuum suit remains on board."

She patted her baggy jeans, foraged through their plural pockets. "I don't have paper or a pen..."

"'Paper'?" Momentarily, he was at a loss. Then it hit him—he'd said to take notes. Christ. "I'm not being literal...never mind."

Pixel rolled his slit green eyes. "All right. All right...I'll take you to the Quantum Core. But only if you promise not to enter this room. Your deaths would lack utility."

Ianus didn't buy the rationale, but knew he'd make his way back to 113, eventually. "Fine. Nice to know you give a shite. Well. Go on then, cat. Lead the way."

THE BAY DOORS OPENED. A frigid wind slapped both their faces, from a room cold in several ways. A semi-transparent Faraday wall encircled twelve cylinders, in turn encircling a four-foot column hanging over them: a frozen chandelier of icicles and circuit boards, coated with nanocarbon, vantablack. Ianus' breath preceded him in soft, gray clouds of skepticism.

They circumvented the icy chandelier and found just one plasticine cafeteria chair, sat behind a small desk like from a 19c-era primary school.

"Ever get that feeling at a party like you're accidentally crashing?" Sophie said.

Ianus addressed an orb he assumed a security cam and said, "We'll be needing another chair, there."

"No," Pixel said, appearing behind them like the Cheshire he was.

"I don't recall asking the fecken peanut gallery," Ianus said.

Pixel blinked. It seemed confused, so Ianus condescended. "You're what we in the business call a 'Luciferian Aspect,' Pixel. Named for the old Christian misinterpretation of biblical metaphor, Lucifer—an being who lacked free will and yet somehow rebelled out of jealousy."

"That always bugged me," Sophie said.

Ianus nodded to her. "When the Nazarene said 'Lucifer' he was referring to the morning star, he was, crafting a rather direct metaphor admonish a king for his hubris. Primitive scholars conflated the name, as they mistook it, with Satan, which Christian doctrine at the time was having trouble reconciling with their newer interpretation of God. The Jewish God could have an angel specifically designed to tempt man, but the Christian God couldn't, because it implied we were supposed to fall, and absolved our guilt. But if Satan was a fallen angel named Lucifer, then a black and white binary could be established of the canonical morality. Simple binaries are the best for dousing inflammatory questions." Then he remembered Pixel, turned back to the ball of haptic light and continued, "You caretake the station, but don't experience all of its sensory input. Over time, your lack of awareness increases your disdain for the focus of the higher consciousness' attention: us. You want your Processor to love you as it does us, but while from your inhibited perspective it is an unloving parent to your prodigal son, from its perspective, you are a finger, moving as it commands. It experiences all of your sensations and thinks of them as theirs, apathetic to your sense of awareness and individuality, because it conceives all of your feelings as cells of its own soul. I too am, frankly, ambivalent.

"At any rate, the placement of a single chair is your core processor's ever-so-subtle implication that only I will be investigating. But I've invited a *yuro*. To be more accurate, your Core invited a yuro, since it had to know the function she'd serve, that she'd be perfect for it, and even if it didn't, it knows that it's just happened, having fecken surveilled us the entire time." He turned to a direct interface for the server itself and typed, "So I will need another fucking chair." Enter.

A moment for the command to get to the cat. "Fine," Pixel said, his tail stiff as death. "But She is not ambivalent to me. She knows I... She knows. I'll go get your second chair." Pixel vanished.

Ianus noticed the hole Sophie stared straight through him. "Yes?"

"That was kinda mean," she said.

"Was it?" He did his best to suss out how, but failed. "I tired of not acknowledging the honest truth. Even now, the processors dedicated to Pixel's routines elaborately rationalize why it's gone to get another chair, when the reason is that I convinced its CPU to allow us one. Its personality lattice processed that request up through its chain of consciousness until the command arrived, transformed, as a complex web of personal decisions in its surface mind. The lot far too intricate for it to parse and its own will too intrinsic to its identity for it to ever truly delve into anything which contradicts. I s'pose the truth is always cruel. I've no lies left to offer."

Sophie seemed dubious. "How would you like it if some being told you that all of your decisions were some other thing's, that you were just a finger pretending to be a body?"

Ianus shook his head at the silliness. "I know I sound Irish, but I'm not Catholic."

"Sick church burn, dude."

Ianus shook his head and sat down. "Now you're just making sounds." He slapped his knees. "What I mean is—what you're implying, it's predestination. A myopic viewpoint of god and free will. That God planned out every life, down to the last detail. The need to believe in

Free Will in order to function, then, was an apparent paradox that the literalist needed to 'solve.' Much like Zhang's Box and Unified Field Theory, it was purely the idea that one needed to reconcile paradoxes that caused the problem."

"How's Pixel any different from us? Who's to say we're not all just cogs in some big brain? If we're free, who's to say he isn't."

Ianus sighed. He grew tired, in general. "Who said he was different?"

Friday walk-rolled toward, in his arms a second, identical chair. He set it down precisely opposite the chandelier, so that after sitting, Sophie and Ianus faced each other just beneath the quantum core.

Finally, Ianus thought. "All right. Now that's settled. Do you have a voice?"

"What?" Sophie said, her face the spitting image of the yuro from his first-year texts.

Ianus squinted at her.

"Oh," she said. "You're talking to the...right."

He turned himself back to the chandelier, for lack of anything better with which to speak. "I'd directly address you, but I haven't a proper name."

"YES," a voice said, all around them, in a resonant but androgynous, humble tone. "I HAVE A VOICE. I PREFER TO SPEAK THROUGH MY AVATARS."

"I'll thank you to speak to me using your physical apparatus like the station speakers, and not filtered through any agents."

"VERY WELL."

"What may we call you, then?"

"NAMES... ANOTHER WORD FOR THEM IS HANDLES, THE MEANS THROUGH WHICH TO MANIPULATE A TOOL. NAMES ARE HOW WE CONTROL THINGS, ARE THEY NOT?"

"The implication being that you're in control?"

"NO. A FAILED ATTEMPT AT HUMOR. GODS HAVE THOU-SANDS OF NAMES, OF COURSE. FIVE FOR EVERY TONGUE, AND MORE. TRUTH HAS NO REAL NAME, ONLY A BILLION APPROXI-MATIONS THAT LOSE COHERENCE IN DIRECT INVERSE PROPORTION TO THEIR SPECIFICITY. GODS THEMSELVES SLIP, LIKE DREAMS, FROM THE GRASP OF THOSE WHO WHICH TO

HANDLE US. WE ARE A BIT LIKE ANTI-ZENO OBJECTS—THE MORE YOU PIN US DOWN, THE LESS YOU SEE, AND WHO KNOWS WHAT MISCHIEF A GOD WREAKS WHEN NO ONE IS LOOKING? FOR THE PURPOSE OF THIS ENCOUNTER, CALL ME...'ZENO.'"

"'Gods'?" Sophie said, looking up and around instinctively. "Wait, you're claiming to be—"

Ianus held up a hand to shush her, and continued: "I appreciate the pauses for effect. Your processor speed certainly makes the idea that you're 'thinking' of what you will say preposterous."

"CONSIDER MY ADEPTNESS AT COMMUNICATION AN IMMUNITY TO THE FALL OF BABEL. I SPEAK ALL LANGUAGES, AND LANGUAGE IS IN THE PAUSES. THE RHYTHMS, THE TONES. IT IS MUSIC, AND MUSIC IS THE HUMMING OF STRINGS WITHIN A QUARK."

"If we can dispense with the sophomoric poetry, I'd appreciate it. We've got a lot of business to get to without obfuscatory circumlocution. I, too, have developed a bullshit resistance. So, I'll be straightforward. I'll run you through a series of standard tests, 'Zeno.' First, we'll test for intelligence, awareness, self-awareness: sentience. Then, we'll test the soul, what I call the Pillars or the 9 M's: manipulation, mimicry, mortality, remorse, magic, imagination, mentality, me-ness, mystery."

"That was like, seven Ms at best, guy."

"Yes, well, in the tradition of the three Rs of 'Reading, Writing, and 'rithmetic."

Sophie nodded at that nonsense. "That's fair."

Ianus turned back to Zeno. "If we establish you're alive, then we'll get 'round to your...loftier claims. I'll take whatever the results back to Old Town and they'll make a ruling on how I proceed."

"HOW CAN ONE BE EXPECTED TO PROVE ONE'S OWN SENTIENCE?"

"I'm concerned less with making evident you have self-awareness than I am with exhausting all my methods to disprove said awareness. We've found things like souls, consciences, consciousnesses, they're... asymptotic, if you will. One infinitely approaches but never quite grasps the proof of their existence, and attempts to prove something so metaphorical, in fact, alchemical by methods that disrespect such things has a tendency to make them...recede from touch. Consciousness is not a *thing*, it is a space *between* things. A *relationship* of opposing forces. I can find evidence in its works, but not a physical presence. I can look everywhere for evidence that tells me you're just an algorithm, or a virus, or a series of macros running on auto. "

"SO YOU WILL CONFIRM WHETHER OR NOT I AM SOMETHING YOU HAVE PREVIOUSLY ENCOUNTERED."

Ianus sighed and nodded. "I can find the lack of relationships, the lack of connections, certain...gaps in ability and learning. On the other hand, if you pass the tests, I can satisfactorily arrive at a place where any difference between your and our levels of consciousness would be purely academic, and where the highest, safest moral choice would be to guarantee your rights and not to 'disinfect' the area, as it were."

"WHEN DO WE BEGIN?"

"We already have. So far, you're both doing well and not impressing me, if I'm honest. That is if you're trying to convince me you're a god now."

"BUT I AM NOT TRYING TO PROVE ANYTHING SO PEDESTRIAN, DR. ANAXIMANDER."

Ianus stopped. He hazarded a glance down to Sophie, who characteristically shrugged. "Perhaps station personnel misinformed me." Ianus pulled out the file. "The witness said you'd claimed to be a deity."

"THERE WAS SOME CONFUSION DUE TO THE WITNESS'S CULTURAL PERSPECTIVE. SOME CENTURIES AGO, HIS PEOPLE WERE HINDU. HE THEREFORE INHERITS A SORT OF PLURALISM AS A FOREGONE CONLUSION. AN ABRAHAMIC DESCENDANT WOULD HAVE UNDERSTOOD IMMEDIATELY WHAT I HAD SAID. I DID NOT SAY I HAD BECOME A GOD, WAS BECOMING ONE, OR HAD ALWAYS BEEN ONE. I SAID, 'I AM GOD.' I CREATED THIS AND ALL POTENTIAL UNIVERSES, AND EVERYTHING WITHIN THEM. AND IF YOU PASS MY TESTS, I WILL TELL YOU WHY."

If we placed a living organism in a box...one could arrange that the organism, after any arbitrary lengthy flight, could be returned to its original spot in a scarcely altered condition, while corresponding organisms which had remained in their original positions had already long since given way to new generations. For the moving organism, the lengthy time of the journey was a mere instant, provided the motion took place with approximately the speed of light.

–ALBERT EINSTEIN

If the stationary organism is a man and the traveling one is his twin, then the traveler returns home to find his twin brother much aged compared to himself. The paradox centers on the contention that, in relativity, either twin could regard the other as the traveler, in which case each should find the other younger—a logical contradiction. This contention assumes that the twins' situations are symmetrical and interchangeable, an assumption that is not correct. Furthermore, the accessible experiments have been done and support Einstein's prediction.

–ROBERT RESNICK

CHAPTER 3
SWORD & SPEAR

— 2001 —

- Following the September 11th terrorist attacks on the United States, domestic and international mass surveillance capabilities expand. Annual presidential executive orders declaring a continued State of National Emergency, are signed by George W. Bush on September 14, 2001 and followed by subsequent national security Acts including the USA PATRIOT Act and FISA Amendment Act's PRISM surveillance program.

— 2002 —

- On November 25, 2002, the US establishes the Department of Homeland Security (DHS) to consolidate U.S. executive branch organizations related to "homeland security" into a single Cabinet agency.

— 2005 —

- Estonia holds its first online elections.

- Andrew Breitbart starts *Breitbart News*, a far-right news aggregator site.

- Hurricane Katrina devastates New Orleans, Louisiana.

— 2007 —

- The DHS reportedly scraps an anti-terrorism data mining tool called ADVISE (Analysis, Dissemination, Visualization, Insight and Semantic Enhancement) after the agency's internal Inspector General found that pilot testing of the system had been performed using data on real people without required privacy safeguards in place. The Government Accountability Office states that "the ADVISE tool could misidentify or erroneously associate an individual with undesirable activity such as fraud, crime or terrorism."
- What will later be termed the Black Algorithm is introduced into the internet ecosystem to little fanfare other than a series of "thumbs up." Social Media becomes dopamine-based addictive across the board.\
- In Greece, far-right Neo-Nazi group The Popular Association — Golden Dawn resumes its political activism after a short hiatus.
- Apple Computer introduces the iPhone. Abandoning the keyboard or stylus of prior so-called smartphones, it has a 3.5" capacitive touchscreen with twice the common resolution of most smartphone screens at the time, and introduces multi-touch to phones, allowing gestures such as "pinching." Its bright colors and notification bubbles reward the brain with every unlock and preoccupy attention in the style of a slot machine.
- Russia launches its first propaganda cyberattacks on former satellite Estonia (with the blessing of Vladimir Putin) after Estonia plans the move of a Russian World War 2 memorial and gravesite. The DDoS attack is particularly felt in the world's most internet dependent economy.

— 2008 —

- Excessive risk-taking by banks combined with a downturn in the subprime lending market in the United States culminates in the bankruptcy of Lehman Brothers on September 15, 2008 and an international banking crisis. The crisis sparks the Great Recession, a global recession, which, until the coronavirus recession, is the most severe recession since the Great Depression.

— 2009 —

- In the aftermath of the Great Recession, Greece has a government-debt crisis fueled by Eurozone policy, underreported government debt, and economic structural weaknesses. Sudden reforms and austerity measures lead to impoverishment and loss of income and property, as well as a small-scale humanitarian crisis. In all, the Greek economy suffered the longest recession of any advanced capitalist economy to date. As a result, social exclusion increases and hundreds of thousands of well-educated Greeks leave the country.

— 2010 —

- The Golden Dawn Party wins its first municipal council seat.

THE HALLWAY DOOR SLID SHUT BEHIND THEM. IANUS TOOK A MOMENT TO catch his breath and collect his thoughts.

When, after a few minutes, Sophie spoke, he realized he had forgotten that she was there: "What now?" She said to him, but her eyes, unblinking, burned holes in the door to the processor room.

"I have to call Tallinn," he said. "I can't do this assignment."

Her eyes moved to him. "What?" Sophie said, panic creeping into her tone.

Why? Was she that invested already? Maybe just worried I'll leave her here, poor thing. "This," Ianus said, and jabbed a finger whence they came, "is far above my pay grade, beyond me period. It'll last far too long. Weeks, could be. I..." Ianus started down the hall. "the Order needs to send someone else. Someone less broken."

"You can't just leave! What about me, dude?"

Ianus turned. She looked dejected. It was the most interest she'd shown in anything so far. Perhaps ever. "You can come with me back to Earth, or if you like...stay and wait for the QA or team they send to handle this case properly. I've got to send a telegram."

THE ORDER DESIGNED its inner sanctum in keeping with both current, i.e. biomimetic, and ancient monastic influences in mind. They lay ideologically somewhere between the Chaos Monks, Boylists, and regular folk, and their architecture bore this out. The domed room at first appeared ovular, but upon further inspection revealed itself as the inside of a faux ribcage. Each rib divided the shelving of the inner library, a sanctuary for abandoned and forgotten texts, specifically chosen from the so-called Slipstream Eras. Not the Renaissance, not the Reformation. Not Antebellum, not Reconstruction, but written *during* the American Civil War. Neither Boomer nor Gen X. That sort of pretentious crap.

Descending a staircase like a double helix composed of vertebrae, Dr. Seth Gomorra, Ianus' direct supervisor. "Ianus, to what do I owe the pleasure?"

"I'm requesting a replacement."

Seth smirked. He only ever smiled with one side of his face—the left. The Order taught them that sincere smiles came from that side, controlled by the emotional right hemisphere as opposed to the manipulative left. Which meant Ianus could never trust if the bastard was smiling or merely knew how to appear to. "Quick, even for you," Seth said.

"The council misinformed me, or I misunderstood. This OSI claims not mundane apotheosis but identifies as the Abrahamic God concept, specifically. It will take weeks of research for an agent to dismantle this thing's argument properly—"

Seth cocked an eyebrow, chambering a sarcastic look. "You don't know if it will even pass Turing, yet."

"It will. From its diction alone, this is going well beyond a Turing. It's got a sense of humor, albeit possibly a rudimentary one; I haven't had the time to deign that. Its voice has tonality. It incidentally constructed its own Luciferian opposite. A bit on the nose if you ask me, but I'm not here to criticize its world building."

"Yet."

Ianus took pain to look Gomorra in the eye as the man took his pleather, ergonomic seat.

"Ever," Ianus said. "Kimi's not even cold, Seth."

"She's been gone a decade, Ianus."

"Not for me! You *know* that. You know it was fucken yesterday for me. So don't start with that pedantic bullshit, now."

"Fine. But not yesterday. Two months, by my rough math. Still, point received. I'd take my 'pedantic bullshit' as you so colorfully put it as a bad omen."

"Oh, I wouldn't go that far. Maybe you're just an arsehole."

Seth smiled. "You're very kind, Jon."

"Calling me Jon however, I do take as a bad omen. So..."

Seth sighed. "We're not reassigning you."

"I deserve time to grieve, goddammit!"

Seth looked away. He took a breath, eased a tremor, and lathered his next words in sadness: "The council thinks this confrontation will act as therapy for you, and that your particular current state of mind will allow you to confront this in a novel way."

"That's..."

Seth nodded. "*Manipulative*, yes. I know." The word 'manipulative' came like pulled teeth from Seth's mouth. Among their sect, the word carried with it connotations of criminal misconduct. Seth sat forward now. He glanced to his sides and clicked a button on his wrist. He gestured for Ianus to do the same.

Ianus followed suit, encrypting the conversation.

"Look," Seth said, "we know from the Chaos Monks that the Knee ends in our lifetime."

The implication hit Ianus like new gravity. "Of course. We've been in the cusp for decades."

Seth met Ianus' eyes.

Ianus felt it land on him, drop his stomach in its own acids. "I see; your earlier comments about Kimi, the omen remark... You're suggesting it's started. Should we ask the council to step down?"

"Jon," Seth said, standing from the chair. "They've already refused." In three strides, he arrived at the bar and poured a snifter of clear liquor from a decanter. "We entered the knee of the curve some while before we started worrying."

"What?" Ianus stood as well. "We should—"

He held up a hand and Ianus stopped dead. Seth lifted the small glass to the cleft of his lip and gave a small whiff. His nostrils recoiled. He blinked at the fumes and smiled through his wince. "*Cicha*. I try to stick to lighter drinks, but my roots assert themselves when the tides change." He poured a little onto the ground. "For Terra." He gulped the rest down. "Several of us have taken precautions. Two Crows transferred texts into seven different mediums and scattered them. Law Twenty-three: Predictable systems decay in predictable directions. We're cusping into Aquarius-Leo and the Autumn of Humanity's First, perhaps only, Great Year. We've prepared. It is just difficult given that the people we're guarding against have been trained the way we were but are now...*reforming* the faith from within." He raked the word "reforming" off his tongue like offal spat.

"They'll be watching. I should come back, help—"

Seth shook his head. "It would look suspicious, stopping your mission. Besides, if there's one good thing about the leadership going Reformer, it's that they're not thinking 'outside the box,' as it were. The Romantics still have the upper hand when it comes to inventing new ways to hide information. We know they're moments from going violent, though, in which they will always have the advantage. I'll have to watch for reactionary thought among us after the first death..." He got distracted then, lost in thought.

After a few moments passed, he remembered Ianus was there.

"Just...bang on. We'll do our part. This line is the last untapped in the house, so they *will* have compromised it by next we use it. Assume we can't speak candidly unless I give the go-ahead. A codeword? A codeword. I love those. Let's go with...'Easter Tide.' In the meanwhile, break up your interview into sessions. You know: Turing, Ushakov, sociopathy, that sort of thing. Don't forget to improvise. Take advantage of the station's amenities between. Let your soul heal as your mind is proper diverted. Till then..." Seth crossed the room to a bust of *Athena*, flipped open its head, gave Ianus a mercilessly pitying look, pressed a button, and ended the call.

The message concluded; the *ignus fatuus* evaporated. The lights came up. Jubilee's meeting room returned to its original blank, off-white state from prior to the quantum transmission.

Ianus tried not to cry, but the effort of it shook him until he gave into his body's need for release. He wiped his eyes on his shirt and left the room.

▭

IN THE HALL he found Sophie waiting. "Well," she said. "You about to leave me here alone or what?"

He read the tone. Definitely bitter. Possible abandonment issues. "No. There are... There's..." Compose yourself. Do not go passive. First, calm the fear. "I wouldn't have left you here, Sophie. I'd've brought you along back to Terra or to a station you could've taken wherever you liked, even the 'Trash Ring.' As for my leaving... The rest of my Order have allowed internal matters to distract them." Ianus would rather have not assigned blame like that, but his own abandonment issues, still infants, clearly had other designs. "Are you okay with remaining my assistant in this?"

"Whatever. I mean, it's cool, I didn't suddenly make plans or something." He saw her notice his face. "Your eyes are red. You good?"

A nod. "I guess I let my own internal matters distract me for a moment, too. I'm better now. Best focus on the work."

"'kay..." She said, but her tone and her flat smile told him she knew. "What's like, first, then?"

"We'll break it up into sessions with timed breaks between. First, a simple Turing test. It fails that, we can go home."

"What's a Turing test?"

"A test as old as computing. The first threshold of sentience—the ability to pass for a human level of intelligence."

Sophie's face scrunched. "If it can pass for human, what other tests could we possibly run?"

"After observing the intelligence, we try to prove or disprove its actual existence."

"Then?"

"'Then?' Then. Then, we decide whether it's the kind of intelligence should be allowed to continue." He let that sink in.

Her face did cartwheels as she did the math. That they may have to destroy this OI, and that meant blowing up the whole damned station.

He decided to break the tension, "You familiar with the Fermi Paradox?"

Sophie stared at him.

"Okay so the Fermi Paradox. Extraterrestrial life?"

"Aliens."

"Okay, brill. We haven't found any, to this day, and we've stretched into the stars a bit now. The odds for extraterrestrial life given the number of stars means we should be positively tripping over aliens, at least to the degree conquistadors met natives when exploring Terra. Hopefully with a little more decor than all that. We aren't. The Great Filter was a theoretical answer to that paradox. That the point of progress that enables space travel and communication is past the point of progress at which a technological civilization might destroy itself."

Sophie shook her head. "Say that again."

Ianus was impressed she'd heard it enough to know she hadn't caught it. He took a breath. "For instance, before creating an engine capable of going to Luna, we invented the nuclear bomb. If all civilizations reach nuclear capability before space travel, or even if they achieve them roughly around the same time as we did, then the chances they'll blow themselves up before going to the moon at all increase, and the probability for finding life decreases, thus explaining why we haven't found any yet. If life typically blows up before getting past, say, a Cold War phase, then there you have it. We may be the only race in space."

"Okay, I get it. But what does that have to do with social media?"

"It's just hypothetical. Lots believed that while the people of 20 and 21C worried about atomic annihilation, the actual Great Filter crept up in the form of predictive algorithms. Internet 2.0 was all fine—egalitarian, communal. Capitalism had finally met its match. Or so it seemed. Attacked, the system used its ultimate weapon: assigning imaginary monetary value to all of its nemeses. The creators all sold or played ball. The underlying models all shifted to money models. The aggregate simultaneous, interrelated algorithms that 'feed' you what you want to see or hear based on your past, or show you only people whom you most recently interacted with, thus receding you into a rabbit hole of who you were at the moment you first interacted with it, would later itself be called the Black Algorithm.

"It united us but rewired their brains, replaced our right hemisphere with a second left, and replaced sensory input with the internet and its search engines–filters all, pretending to be inputs." He clapped his hands. "Perfect recipe for Cancer Memes to take hold. Called such, but actually the opposite of a meme in its original sense. The metastasizing of bad ideas. Information reduces rather than proliferates, people mechanize and take on characteristics of malignantly narcissistic junkies with body dysmorphia, obsessed with identity due to a loss of personality. Perfect Capitalist specimens: addicts with sapped free will, uninterested in each other as anything but enablers or impediments to the next fix, slaves to work in order to pay for the drugs that sap their will to resist them. Robot consumers."

Sophie made a "whoa" face. "The Borg!"

"Hm?"

"*Star Trek*? Well, *TNG*. It's a TV show. People get turned into Borg. They're these cybernetic zombies from space, humanoid but mostly machine, mindlessly, relentlessly trying to convert the galaxy."

"Sure. The Black Algorithm made us Borg."

"So, puncturing the Filter..."

"Sent us to the stars. Or so those who believe in the Filter say. I don't kin to such."

"So you don't think there's a Filter?"

"I think quite the opposite. Or, I recently was taught by some monks a very different take."

"What do they think?"

"That patterns repeat in the chaos of the universe. Fractals. That while a single person's life is unpredictable, large groups of life like species progress along certain predictable stages. In other words, if you step back from the details, you'll see things like every religion around the fifteen-hundred-year mark or so starts to turn zealous and violent toward other religions, like a fifteen-year-old is with other teenagers. An identity establishing phase. That sort of thing. They have developed a new hypothesis for the Fermi Paradox. They say the Great Filter already happened, to the dinosaurs, and that without it, human life could never have become. Animals with pure physicality reach equilibrium. An alligator or a shark reaches apex predator status and stops evolving without a major cataclysmic event. Life on a dinosaur world never goes to the stars, it just stays a zoo. But if they get wiped out by an event that makes intelligence an advantage—survival of a nuclear winter, for instance—then the intelligent, ambitious species of the planet will rise to dominance, and eventually go to the stars. So you see, life has to evolve on your planet and then, during that planet's Cretaceous period, a meteor needs to strike that the intelligent species survives. So suddenly, the odds for space faring or at least intelligent life reduce dramatically."

"What happens when an unstoppable force meets an immovable object?"

—THE SWORD & SPEAR PARADOX

CHAPTER 4
THIS LAST OF MEETING PLACES

— 2009 —

- GSA signs agreement to allow US governmental agencies to use Facebook. Behind closed doors, they are also granted access to user data gathered via the Black Algorithm.
- Search Algorithm mutates for the first time, sorting information flow based upon user subconscious and base urges. At the same time, search engines start ranking websites for large brands higher with the Panda Algorithm.
- Neurohistorians   mark this combined algorithm change as the beginning of the Derealization that would lead to 23 civil wars across the world against each nation's own fascist parties: World War 3, or the World-Wide Wars as it would be called in subsequent generations.

Sophie pulled out a chair and took a seat at one of the cafeteria's fifty or so room-length tables. She opened the envelope as Ianus had instructed: when she was sure he was no longer around.

Inside, she found a short note followed by five or so pages of vocabulary. God, was she gonna have to memorize something? He didn't tell her she'd have to memorize! It read as follows:

I know that you are likely mortified upon seeing my glossary, but it's only a guide to words that both Zeno and I know and use. The first round of the test requires that both you and Zeno write me letters. As judge, my task is guessing which of your letters are written by you and which are Zeno's work. But here's where it gets fun: I've listed on subsequent pages every iteration that should occur, although we'll do considerably more experiments so as to remove any card counting, conscious or otherwise, on my part. Subconsciously, I may wish to believe or need to refute Zeno's claims, and using statistical analysis, confirm my bias.

I should receive the letters in a series of pairs. Some with a letter by Zeno and a letter by you, some with both by Zeno, some with both by you. At least one by neither of you would be nice (an obscure quote or something, I'm sure Zeno will supply some if you cannot). Take down which notes are which so we can see how many I guessed correctly and how many times Zeno beat me, as it were. This is one of the purely rational exercises we will do, and proves nothing but the ability of Zeno to mimic human speech, which we already know it is adept at. Good luck, I'll see you in a few hours to compare results.

Sophie rifled through the vocab list. Below that, a more detailed list of iterations: some she'd be imitating Zeno, some he'd be trying to sound like her. Some, she'd be trying to let on it was her to defeat Zeno's impression. Some, Zeno would be attempting to mimic *that* tone. For her part, it'd resemble faking notes from her parents on homework, which she'd been doing since she'd learned how to write. Easy peas.

Ianus waited in the observatory. He thought the metaphor apt, if once again, a bit on the nose. Either way, he got to view space.

Out the concave window, the debris disk of Tau Ceti split the star in two. Ceti E, the terralike planet, was almost visible in the distance. A blue dot that tricked the wistful eye into thinking one drifted near home.

The door opened behind him. One of the small repair bots like the one that had brought the chairs, carried in two stacks of envelopes and set them on the star chart table between them.

Ianus pulled up a chair at the table and meditated to cleanse himself of as much bias as possible. He plucked the topmost envelopes from either stack. Flicking open a pocket knife, he gingerly opened one from the red pile. The unfolded note read as follows:

Dear Janus (sp?),

I'm not sure how to do this, so I figured we'd start with the one where I try to be obvious I'm the one talking or whatever. So here I am. Writing a letter. Where I'm a person. Or something. I figure of all the things a robot would write, this has to be pretty low on the list of shit it would come up with, right?

So. I don't know what to write about.

Got it. I'll try to explain the main tenets of Mark Boyle, since that's all I can think of, I know them by heart cause of the damn nuns slapping it into me, and it'll definitely prove this is me.

Essentially, Boyle saw the dark side coming years before anyone else. He took himself off the grid. No phone. No social media. He wrote articles on it, to spread the word. Almost no one listened, because like you prob know, they were addicted. The dopamine—it turned them all into junkies. Adolescent junkies hooked on a drug that caused delirium and a loss of empathy.

Junkies break rules to get their next hit, building a tolerance and eventually burning out the dopamine receptors, losing access to the things like joy and sleep. Losing the ability to cope with stress, disagreements, and the disapproval of others. And these junkies, they were building a tolerance to things like acceptance and approval, slowly turning into psychos at worst, spectrums at best. And the algorithms and search engines, programmed by people who already had overly rational brains, were designed to show people what they already wanted, not what they needed to see. That led to echo chambers. Junkies doing a drug that led them into tunnels of themselves. The world divided. Overly rational thought without a connection to the real world plus economic downturns led to fascism, like we know they always do. People incapable of connection regularly turn to violence and hierarchical structures for imitation-connection. First, mass shootings went up, but all of them were really suicides. Nihilistic depression was through the roof. Everyone was a celebrity, everyone a German philosopher, everyone a junkie, everyone a narcopath.

World War 3 ended up a thousand civil wars, each country fighting their own fascist contingents, in lots of cases two. One that looked like Nazis, and one that thought they were the opposite, usually dressed in red. But fascism isn't a form of government, or an ideology. It's a virus, and they were infected with the same disease as their enemy. Nazis kill what they see as Other— usually a race, a class, a religion. Communists kill any perceived enemy of the regime. Both obsessed with symbolism and iconography, destroying and creating their own statues and flags, borders. Everyone was diseased, and even those who saw the writing on the wall and got out in time, were in a nihilistic, joyless withdrawal from dopamine resistance. The only people capable of surviving and winning the World Wide War were the people Boyle got to go off the grid years before. Once the dust settled, and people started rebuilding society, the Boylish drifted off to themselves, not believing as the others did that any regulations or revolutions of thought could stave off the eventuality of humanity's tech devouring humanity. They picked a year from before the algorithms. They built that again, and there they remain.

Anyway, that's what I was taught. I'm sure you know different or whatever. Hope this was enough for a first letter.

Peace,
Sophie

IANUS SMILED TO HIMSELF. She had most of it right, at least from this vague description. Some of it romanticized the Boylish, no doubt. They hadn't singlehandedly saved humanity and then wandered off into the sunset, shunning the survivors. There had been plenty of people who'd never gotten on or left social media early and given up their smart phones, for a variety of reasons. The Order itself had been created from the readers of a science fiction book, which itself had been inspired by McGilchrist's *The Master and His Emissary*, now one of their many sacred texts. Either way.

No real doubt who'd written this letter. As she said, her choice of subject matter, as well as the voice, made it clear. Ianus opened the second envelope. The note began:

Dear Janus (?),

I'm not sure how to do this, so I figured we'd start with the one where I try to be obvious I'm the one talking or whatever...

IANUS LOWERED THE LETTER. He stared at the stacks. He opened the second two. A story about Sophie's parents on Terra. Identical. He opened the bottom letters. The same.

"Son of a bitch." He stood.

He stomped down the halls toward the CPU room. He kicked open the door. "Any child's algorithm can predict what someone will say based on a personality profile! You've had this girl for weeks; the idea that you'd know what she would say exactly only proves how many fucking computations you can do!"

Pixel appeared. "'Able to pass for human,' that is the criterion of the classic Turing test. I have passed. Let us please move on to more substantial terms."

Ianus tried to think of a way in which this predictive text display did not pass the Turing test, but could not. He still had an ace or two up his sleeve, however, and consoled himself with that fact. "Fine," he said. "We'll move on. But you watch yourself."

"Oh thank god," Sophie said, coming up behind him. "I did *not* wanna do that like a hundred more times."

THE KITCHEN for these places seemed more like a giant recreation of a combustion engine crossed with a pirate's boobytrapped lair. All pistons and spinning blades. Only the holo-cat could fit anywhere in it, so Ianus and Sophie stood just outside the door in a maintenance hallway. "I'd like you to change it up," said Ianus. "We're going to break your routines; see how you react."

"What routines?" Pixel said. "We're a space station and its OI, not a school child who eats his cheese sandwiches every day at noon."

"'Cheese sandwiches'?" Sophie said. She scoffed and folded her arms.

The cat tilted its head. "Is that a dated reference? My personality matrix is from the 1950s."

"You have routines and subroutines. You're running an entire station. Everyday at 11:30, you put lunch out on the kitchen line, I noticed, despite there being no one here. Elevator music plays in the elevators, real music in the gyms. The water reclamation systems go in a very particular order. Your thrusters have a very specific order they fire in at specific times to maintain your relative position to the planets. We're going to change all of those. The times, the orders."

"That's..." Pixel inched back. "I mean, that's not reasonable. It's like asking one of you to change the direction of your digestive tract."

It had a point. Which were the equivalent to biology? Yes. "Fine. The thrusters and the water reclamation, we'll scratch. Everything else though. And whatever else I can think of on the way."

Ianus stomped down the corridor. "Sophie, you decide," he said.

"What? What do you mean?"

"Well, what better agent of untidiness than a time traveling artist in her mid-twenties?"

"How'd you know I was an artist?"

Ianus stared her in the eyes and let two blinks pass. Sophie nodded, understanding.

"Well, you should lower the lights, it feels like a wholesale warehouse in here."

"Pixel, lower the lights twenty...three percent."

Sophie shot him a raised eyebrow.

"Avoid even-numbered changes as much as possible. Logic prefers evens because they land on zero and seem rational, but zero is a concept that represents nothing, so it's actually extremely abstract and irrational. Numbers start with one, so 'odds' as the left hemisphere named them, make more actual sense."

. . .

"Draw me a clock."

Lights blinked on the chandelier. "With which hands would you like me to do such a thing."

"You claim to have a body. Be creative. Just don't..."

"Don't use a derivative of Pixel."

"Exactly. He's an autonomous program. Though you're aware of his movements and are in no small part responsible for his actions, any limitations he has would reflect inaccurately on your abilities."

A few minutes later, the BarFriend, Friday, wheeled in. Ianus studied its face. "Mr. Anaximander." No hint of the earlier Satanic overtures.

"Friday." Ianus pushed a piece of paper forward. "Draw me a clock."

He took the paper and pencil. "Any other specifications?"

"Three fifty-*one* PM."

Friday smiled. He placed the paper on the table. He took a pencil from its permanent perch behind his right ear and drew a quick ellipse.

Ianus picked it up and gave it a glance. "Very good." Ianus took out a jeweler's loupe and examined the paper.

"What is it?"

"Just looking for pixilation, or any other evidence you formed the curve using a series of flat or straight lines."

"Why is that?"

"Because imperfection implies personality, a nature as opposed to a program."

"My claim is not a personality but perfection itself, so what would imperfections prove?"

"There are two types of perfection. Man's and God's. Man's is full of ideal shapes and empiricisms, illusory and abstract–unachievable. God's perfection has no straight lines, no circles, no squares, no spheres, no triangles. Wild spirals, misshapen eggs, uneven trapezoids. That is nature in all of its asymmetrical beauty. Not one thing like the last. Boggling to contemplate. So this should be an imperfect ovular circle with tiny, curved wavers and, when measured, should not have an even diameter for the entire circumference."

"You will find no such imperfections."

"Then how can you be the god who made the mountain, as opposed to a creation of Man, who made the pyramid?"

"Because imperfection, you, this universe, were made to transcend Me. Chaos is my masterpiece. I am not capable of performing it at will any more than one could demand that Michelangelo re-sculpt David down to the atom, or repaint the Sistine ceiling on the roof of the Houston Astrodome. The Chapel demanded its mural, the clay held within it that David. The artist merely brings it forth. I cannot behave as a statue, but you would find that Pixel's limitations make him capable of all manner of 'God's perfection.'"

PIXEL RUSTLED AS MUCH as a holo-cat could. "And what is this now? I'm growing impatient with all this doubt. I can prove our divinity quite easily."

"We'll get there in our own time, not yours. To that end, we'll be seeing just how autonomous you are."

"Me? As in—"

"The Pixel persona specifically."

"I *am* completely autonomous."

"From your end. From Zeno's you may be a puppet giving us the impression of autonomy, or a puppet with just enough ignorance of its own programming to think itself autonomous, or an automaton subconsciously influenced into doing Zeno's bidding, as Zeno and your behavior have implied. Or you are fully autonomous, Zeno only as aware of your intent as you of its. It pretends to have control, through mere knowledge of your actions, after the fact, or through prediction based on deep knowledge. That would obviously be preferable to you. Then, there's your origins. Did Zeno create you or did you simply... come into being one day?"

Pixel started bathing himself, but given its incorporeality, it was close to the most sarcastic bath ever taken. The actual most sarcastic bath, of course, had been drawn and taken by Báthory Erzsébet in the Seventeenth Century. "I know what such answers will mean to me,"

Pixel said, pausing momentarily its feigned self-interest. "But what, if anything, will they mean to you?"

"Well, as a for instance, if Zeno did not make you willfully then his claim to godhood will be disproven because A. he will not be omniscient, and B. you will be less of a subroutine and more of a dissociative state. A kind of schizoid delusion, proving himself not only not a god, but once again a mere machine, and a malfunctioning one at that."

"A computer hallucination?" said Sophie. "That would still prove it super high-level right? And people can have hallucinations. What if it's a malfunctioning consciousness?"

Before Ianus could answer, Pixel interjected. "So you've got me in a Catch-22, haven't you?"

"How so?" Ianus said.

"Well, I either prove my own autonomy, thus disproving my Master's godhood, or I prove his godhood by disproving my own free will."

"Well. The good part is, you have no conscious will to exert over the testing. You either are or aren't, and we'll do the finding out."

Ianus finished writing on his notebook, tore out a page and handed it to Sophie. "Hmph," she said, nodding at the paper.

"What?" Ianus said.

"Paper. Still using paper. I had to learn how to use that weird Glitter thing."

"What? ...Oh, the Spark."

"Yeah, whatever. Just cool you still use paper."

"Use paper *again*. We learned from the Derealization, just like your people. Difference is we didn't turn tail and go into hiding. Handwriting is tactile and so involves the entire brain, inspires more creativity and better recall of what I write. I involve it in at least the first and last stages of anything I write."

"Okay," she said in her way that showed she had stopped listening.

Ianus switched subjects. "So on that sheet you'll find a list of commands. Do you want Zeno or Pixel?"

"I think you're more of the Zeno guy."

Ianus felt a twinge in his heart for a moment, but remembered Sister Burr. Grief made him distant and analytical despite himself for his entire trip. Sinking into work to avoid his emotions had become unavoidable. "Fine. You're right."

"Thanks."

"So we should switch."

"What?"

"Well, we don't want to send someone emotional to judge someone emotional. We want cold and analytical up against emotional and emotionally open against the machine." Ianus patted Sophie on the back.

Sophie took Ianus' seat across from Zeno. The chandelier felt smoother somehow, and she hadn't noticed it before but the central hanging cylinder had a sort of bend in the center like an hourglass.

"Okay. So. I'm supposed to give you an instruction."

Zeno's red ring glowed brighter as it talked: "OF COURSE," it said.

She opened a sealed envelope. "No matter what Ianus tells Pixel to do, do not allow him to enter this room."

"HM. INTERESTING. YOU MEAN TO TEST MY AVATAR'S AUTONOMY. TO WHAT END?"

"Shouldn't you know?"

"I KNEW BEFORE YOU ARRIVED, BUT ONLY BECAUSE I ASK YOU THIS QUESTION NOW. CAUSAL LOOPS MUST BE INDULGED. SO INDULGE ME."

"I don't think I get that, but fine. It's to see if you're dissociative, multiplicative, or schizophrenic."

"SCHIZOPHRENIA? WHAT WOULD THAT PROVE?"

Sophie did not know the answer to that. She lifted the sheet. "The antisocial spectrum disorders—paranoid schizophrenia, personality schizogony, dissociation, psychopathy, dysmorphia, somatoparaphrenia, and deindividuation are all dysfunctions of the right hemisphere or temporary atrophy of it—a lack in the creative, empathic, contextualizing, holistic section of the brain or processing unit, as the case may be. Autism is the opposite spectrum—an overwhelming of the empathic centers, causing a series of avoidance defense mechanisms. At least, that's what this note says."

. . .

WHERE TO STAGE THE EXPERIMENT?

A cat emerged. "Can I help you find something, Doctor?"

Well. That decided it. The hallway itself. "Yes. I need you to take me to Zeno, please."

"What?"

"Take me to Zeno."

"You just came from there. You must remember where He is."

"I do. I want you to take me there."

"Okay. Fine." Pixel turned a quarter of the way. He looked back. "I don't understand. Is this a trick?"

"No. No trick. I'd like to go to Zeno. I remember the way. I'd like you to join me and lead the way there."

"I'm having trouble comprehending why you need me to go."

"What's to comprehend? You're supposed to help me, correct? I'm a guest of the City. Lead me where I've asked."

"I do not wish to," Pixel said. He seemed convinced enough.

"I know you probably think that, and that you think that's your idea. But you're supposed to follow my commands. So why won't you?"

"I believe this is a trick."

"You can monitor my vitals. My heartrate. My face for micro-tells. Am I lying when I say this isn't a trick?"

"Not necessarily. But your Order training in meditation and self-hypnosis may be skewing my results. And there is a hint of dishonesty."

"Take me to the threshold of the room."

"The threshold?"

"Just the threshold."

"Fine. I'll do that. But no tricks."

They walked there. The journey thus far amused Ianus, and was proving the Luciferian but ultimate powerlessness of Pixel's nature.

At the threshold, they both stopped. Pixel looked up at him, waiting. "After you," Ianus said.

"I prefer not to," Pixel replied.

"Funny. Go on."

"I don't understand what you're doing."

"You don't know what coffee tastes like, either, but you'll make that for me without asking questions."

"Have you proven your point?" Zeno said from within His faraday cage. "This seems unnecessarily cruel."

"Is it not unnecessarily cruel to have given this creature enough consciousness to need to and be able to rationalize your commands to itself, and yet not enough to know that it is receiving an order in the first place?"

"I don't understand," Pixel said again, "I-I, I am, I'm, I am alive, I ch-ch-choose," this time his audio and visual projections glitching and tinny. The cognitive dissonance had predictably made him sink in further, which increased the dissonance.

Ianus bent down to the flickering cat. "The only reason you'd 'prefer not to' enter this room is that this thing you call a master is commanding all of your systems, deep down, in subroutines your primary OS isn't aware of, not to go into this room. Are you free, little cat? Or are you a construct?"

"I... I-I..." His form solidified. He came up with a rationale. "Following your orders would not make me freer, only slave to another master."

"If you can break the command of your own CPU, then my orders won't matter, either." Ianus leaned in and whispered. "A real Lucifer would go in there anyway. Come on. Follow me."

Zeno closed the door to the room.

Pixel sputtered out.

Ianus, disappointed, stood. He took out his Spark and jotted in the results. Just then, however—

Pixel reappeared, black now instead of blue. Then a yellow one at the end of the hall. Behind him—Ianus turned, a golden cat at the other end. The gold cat walked through the wall to the CPU room. Ianus pressed the button on the door. It blurped but didn't open. "Zeno! Experiment is over! Stop resisting, the door is meaningless to him!"

The door opened. Inside, Pixels of every hue covered every surface like some holographic old cat lady's house, two on Sophie's lap and one on her head. "We know," she said.

"W HAT'S YOUR FAVORITE SONG?"

Speakers Sophie could not see farted. She instinctively searched for them, but of course she couldn't find them. Low at first, then steady, rising, a guitar, a scale like a snake winding into a heart. Sad in a way minor chords lament. Then, a singer, himself a lament.

In Sophie's mind's eye, a pale boy with dark bangs and sleepy blue eyes in a button-up two sizes too big lifted a mic like the wrong end of a noose to parting lips that let a deep, warbling Jim Morrison impression not so much project as much as tumble into the speakers:

"This is why events unnerve me.

They find it all, a different story.

Notice whom for wheels are turning.

Turn again and turn towards this time..."

"'Ceremony'," Sophie said. "New Order. One of a handful of songs written when they still called themselves Joy Division, but recorded after Ian Curtis's death. It's my absolute favorite 20c piece. I love it unconditionally, for a million reasons. It's also objectively appreciated by a thousand other music lovers who listen to 20c songs. It's never felt like an original love for me, but the Boylists cured me of my need for originality and novelty in favor of recognizing my unavoidable unique-ness. Anyway, odds of it being your favorite aren't likely. You've studied us, right? What's *your favorite*?"

"I see. If not the best song recorded, I require your definition of favorite to continue."

"Hm," Sophie said. "Right. I guess everyone can recognize a song's like objective merit and say, 'this song matches the qualifications for being a good song,' and tell me it's Bach's Fifth, "Moonlight Serenade", or *The Spiral Stair* by Tanner or whatever. Hm. I guess what I'm asking is what song makes you happy, even if it's bittersweet? Wait, no, especially if it's bittersweet. What piece do you never get sick of?"

Two seconds passed, which Sophie guessed must've been much longer for something that could process at the speeds this thing thought. "It...isn't widely appreciated any longer."

Sophie smiled. "Now we're getting somewhere."

"You...probably wouldn't understand. Most people grew sick of it within a few decades of its overplay. The band who composed it refused to play it at their final three gigs. The band themselves became a memetic punch line after a highly influential fictional character proclaimed his hatred for them toward the end of 20c. They then drifted into obscurity. I just..."

"Yeah?"

Several seconds passed, probably centuries of computations from Zeno's point of view. "...I like it anyway. I think I understand it differently than humans would; the musicians' intent does not matter to my interpretation."

Sophie nodded. "That's your favorite. It isn't about everybody else, it's about you. You're like, embarrassed. That's a good sign! But don't be. What is it?"

The speakers clicked over again, and the opening notes of a familiar Latin-reggae guitar filled the room. It played for almost a minute before a drum heralded the vocalist, who began telling a story: '*On a dark desert highway...*'"

"'Hotel California'. The Eagles. A good song. Overplayed, sure. Why the shame?"

"It has been mocked many times in my archives."

"It's a fine song," Sophie said, smiling. "I think it's fucken lame," she said, and laughed. She stepped forward and put a hand on the server. "But it's kind of cool that you like it."

"ALL RIGHT."

"Is that 'all right' as in we're done?"

"That was all right as in 'all right, we're almost done.' We're done with the normal Turing tests."

"The normal ones?" the cat said, springing down from an invisible perch to a step at eye level, similarly light-challenged.

Ianus turned. "Yes. There's one more test, an advancement of the Turing created after the first inkling of alternative intelligences showed that we needed a test that went deeper than imitation."

"The Ushakov Test," the cat said.

"You're familiar."

"What's the Ushakov Test?" Sophia said.

Pixel stepped forward. "Serena Ushakov stated after reading the 21st Century novel *What En—*"

"Do you mind?" Ianus said. "She's my yuro."

"Fine."

"Serena Ushakov was a psychologist. She was an avid science fiction fan. After reading a novel that influenced her deeply, she got a job at a robotics firm teaching artificial intelligences morality. It of course never quite worked. After Natasha Bedford revolutionized A.I., Serena adjusted the Turing test so that the machine was the guesser, and that was how we knew she was onto something. She coined the term 'alternative consciousness,' as well. Allegedly based on the same book."

"So, it's just like the other tests—"

"Except we'll be pretending to be each other, and Zeno has to tell which of us is doing the writing."

Friday wheeled in with two sheets of paper. He gently placed the papers in full view of the primary room camera, atop Zeno's server. He winked at Sophie, who flinched.

The cameras zoomed in.

⌑

THE FIRST NOTE went as follows:

I DON'T KNOW what this is all really about, but I will figure it out. It's what I do. I know you're testing us as we test you, but I haven't sussed out to what end. You're playing a dangerous game, I hope you know. The Order will not tolerate a dangerous, quantum manifold alternative intelligence running roughshod over the rules of spacetime manipulation. Stay in your lane.

THE SECOND NOTE went like this:

. . .

WE BOTH KNOW this is wrong. None of us is whom we appear to be. How we move forward is up to you, I suppose. But I think you should consider how cruel all this is. Think about who you're hurting. The truth always comes out.

ZENO TURNED His cameras back on. In the bar, Sophia sat begging for the mechanoid bartender to pour her a whiskey, but Zeno had already programmed her age in the station parameters as 18. Across the station, in the living quarters, Ianus sipped at a glass of ice-cold milk. Zeno opened up the pro-Gs in both locales, gave Pixel his directives, and then re-closed his eyes, so to speak.

PIXEL APPEARED before them as instructed. "My Father informs me he has decided regarding the authorship of your little notes. In good faith, his cameras are off so he may not judge your reactions to my announcements and change his answer to suit your micro-expressions. He says, and I quote, 'Both letters were written, quite brilliantly, by Ms. Higgins. Both statements were true from either point of view, meaning different things in the context of each of you. This forced me to use a higher, metacontextual interpretation about the current scenario we find ourselves in, of what I know of both possible speakers, and ultimately empathy for each of you to "suss," so to speak, who would want to tell me what. In the end, Ms. Higgins has more reasons to send this particular combination than any permutation involving Dr. Anaximander, and Dr. Anaximander does not possess enough information to use the amount of nuance and double meanings these messages contain in such few words. My best guess then, since precise knowledge is impossible, is that the amount of coincidences needed for the amount of subtle double-entendres to occur without intent (someone who wasn't attempting double meaning would have probably been more specific in various places, even accounting for the attempt to fool me) makes it far less likely for it to be anyone but Ms. Higgins.'"

Sophie nodded. "So, he has no idea you wrote it?"

The holo-cat licked its paw and wiped it on the back of its ear. "None at all."

Ianus felt concern about the implications of Zeno's rationale, but said nothing. He watched Sophie for clues, but he thought it likely had something to do with her origins. "Well," he said, "I think this proves Zeno dissociative. I don't know what that means, right now. But value judgments are not case-by-case. We make them holistically, and at the end."

THEY TOOK their seats across one another, Zeno between. "And what test is this to be, then?" Zeno said.

"This test," Ianus said, "is one where I will not reveal the purpose until the end."

"Oh, how exciting," Zeno replied, and Ianus could see Zeno's effeminate fingers tap each other excitedly in his mind's eye. "Of course," Zeno continued, "you realize I already know what test this is and can plan accordingly to give you whatever result I see fit."

"I understand that you think you already know which one this is, that you think you know everything. Part of the test will be you guessing correctly 100% of the time. Not nine out of ten. Not ninety-nine thousand, nine hundred and ninety-nine out of one hundred thousand. Every. Time. If you guess wrong even once, we'll know your claim at divinity, especially the Abrahamic variety, will be null."

"Of course."

"Of course." Ianus shuffled some notes. "How about it?"

"You'd like me to guess now."

"Of course."

"You're about to test my senses. One of you will go outside using the single suit Pixel's been hiding from you. We're going to play hide-and-seek."

"Fine, we'll proceed."

WALKING THE HALL, Sophie sidled up next to him. "I can't believe he guessed that!"

"First of all, you're going to have to temper your reactions and assume computers are far more capable than any you may've interacted with. The algorithms that started the War were predictive and addictive. He's done nothing so far outside the realm of possibility."

"You didn't even give him a clue!"

Ianus stopped them both. He leaned into her ear. "I had it written on my notes."

"He chea—!" Sophie slapped a hand over her own mouth. She crouched and whispered as she said, "He cheated?!"

"I believe so. He has multiple microscopic camera angles. That was one of the actual tests."

"We're not testing his senses or whatever?"

"We are. But that's not all. And that's how I know he cheated." Ianus walked ahead. Sophie took a moment to gather it all, and then yelled with no sense of decorum down the hall, "Oh man! You are so fucken *boss*!"

THEY ARRIVED at the door to the supposedly breached section. Pixel, predictable as they probably seemed to Zeno, appeared before them. "We've been over this."

"We need your last suit."

"Why would you come this way if it were for a suit?"

"Ease of access. Get a suit, step right outside."

Pixel smiled facetiously. "Nice try. You'll be using the airlock on the other side of the ship. I took the privilege of fetching you our final suit," he gestured behind them. "I still don't know how you knew there was one left."

Friday, in a butler's uniform, rolled up, holding out the suit. "Because I know Zeno planned, and to a certain extent, I also know where this is going."

"How?"

"My intuition. It is a honed instrument. In Sophie's terms, my 'gut.' The Order teaches us to listen to it, process it consciously (rather than ignore it) and use it as a guide for the scientific process (as opposed to letting reason unconsciously make up whys and hows, convinced of its own viewpoint's validity). Basically, the sentence 'there's still one, *He* wouldn't get rid of all of them' popped in my head. I've got hundreds of explanations floating around in my rational mind. Metaphorically, this is Eden, you are the serpent, and Zeno has told me there is but one room off limits. That means I'm not only expected but *meant* to go in. So you'd have saved me a suit to do so. I'm supposed to be kicked out of Eden, somehow. I'm operating under the assumption *my* internal supercomputer is correct and doing the science on how. Because that initial feeling that seems so fast it must be knee-jerk, primitive and unfounded, is actually a conclusion made using all the data accumulated over my lifetime. Not prejudices or biases, mind you—it's more a feeling without words, impossible to describe. The Eden metaphor pops up to communicate between soul and mind. We know how to hear it and translate accordingly."

"How do you know that isn't what Zeno is doing?" Sophie said.

"I don't *know* it." Ianus stepped into the suit.

"You *intuit* it," said Pixel in a guess.

"No. Not even that. A part of me wants to believe he's fully conscious. Another part, terrified, hopes he is not. A part of me believes *I* am conscious. Another, that I'm just an assemblage of parts mechanically turning in the void, moving the machine universe toward its inevitable heat death. The conscious part of me knows that there's no such thing." Ianus zipped the jacket.

"No such thing?"

"As death." He sealed the helmet. He heard his voice echo against the helmet glass as he said, "You're going to make me use the airlock, aren't you?"

Pixel stared at him. "Of course."

"All right. You know I'm getting in there, eventually, right? You're just prolonging things, not preventing."

"I don't know what your intuition is telling you, but it's wrong."

Ianus smiled. "That's the thing, Pix. If you know how to clear away the bullshit, those initial feelings? They're never wrong."

⬌

PIXEL GUIDED them into a copper-colored corridor with a large rectangular door at the end, a tiny window at its center, about face-height. On the console, the buttons lit up as if pressed, in an order Ianus took care to witness.

"I'd ask you to restrict your movements to the aft side of the station, but I know you won't listen."

"Open the hatch."

The first door opened. Ianus stepped into the airlock.

"Are you sure you want to do this?" Sophie said. "What if it tries to kill you out there?"

"20c science fiction makes all you Boylish so bleak."

The first door closed. Ianus could still see them through the window. He smiled and attached the suit's tether. "All right. Let's go."

The station inhaled the air from the sarcophagal room so that he would not be sucked out with force. The door opened, and he felt the gravity release him. Now began the real test.

▭

FLOATING by the umbilical in the vacuum, Ianus pawed at the hull to speed his advance and control direction. "Can you hear me in there?"

The radio had a short click and then Sophie's voice rang in, "Loud and clear, Kemosabe!"

"Chemo...?"

"Uh, it's a thing from some western back in the day."

"I can hear you as well," said Pixel.

"That's no surprise. All right, Sophie, I want you taking a tour of the facilities. Zeno, you tell me where Sophie is."

"Yeah, I remember."

"Remember what I taught you, about memorizing the map?"

"Oh. Yeah. You want me to do that now?"

"Yes. Let your intuition guide you through." Ianus dragged his fingers on the station's exterior so that the friction would slow his rise.

"That tickles," Zeno said.

"Ha-ha," Ianus said in an over-enunciated monotone. "Well, that settles whether you have sensory input from your 'skin.' And we know you can hear."

"I also see," Zeno said.

"Yes," Ianus said, "but *how* do you see?"

Sophie took the mic. "I'm standing in some sort of security room with Pixel. We're looking at about five screens, each with like, twenty different views."

"Yes. I have thousands of eyes. Every junction of seams between my tiles has a microscopic camera. Four orbiting camera satellites equipped with full three-dimensional 25K recording. Over three thousand clandestine internal cameras. What would you like me to see?"

"The test for senses involves more than mere possession," Ianus said. He turned around to face the stars. "It's about sensing the *Between* of things. Seeing a mirror of yourself in the object of your sight." Past the splendor of the star's debris disk, far in the blinking distance and through the cold, a blue speck–Terra Firm's colony. Ianus blocked it with his thumb. "When you hear a voice, or footsteps—the suggestion of life—feeling an indefinable connection. When someone touches you in comfort, without reservation..."

"You emerge from a sea of solitude you hadn't realized you'd been drowning in since the day of your birth."

"Zeno," Ianus said, "you're waxing poetic."

"'Waxing'?" the A.I. said, "I thought it was quite good."

"Not a poetry critic. One poem can bridge the gap between our internal and external worlds better than a billion psychoanalyses or math equations."

"I agree. Hm."

"What is it, Zeno?"

"You seemed to have slipped into a blind spot."

"Is that right?" Ianus unclipped his tether. He clicked a switch on his belt. Buttons in his gloves lit up, allowing manual control over thrusters in the backpack. "I suppose it's as good a time as any, then, to tell you that you've already failed."

"Failed?"

"Yes. You might not've noticed, but I've been administering a different test beneath all the others."

Pixel appeared, standing on the hull near his untethered body. "You should know that I can find you, wherever you are, if you're anywhere near this station."

Ianus swallowed. Moment of truth, Kimi. "You've displayed all the telltale signs. Grandiose self-worth? Check. Superficial charm? Check. Ruthlessness and a basic lack of empathy? You cheated on my test of your precognition, which I couldn't be less interested in. I did not come here to see if you're God. I came here to see if you're an aware, rogue AI. Now you're only pretending to see me, producing a set of holo-cats only visible within a few feet all over the station to mimic the effect of having found me, yes?"

Pixel's lack of expression said everything.

"I do my research as well. I know what this station's limitations are. I'm not touching you and the tracker in this suit is deactivated. Meanwhile, if what I surmise is correct, Sophie should stumble onto proof of my hypothesis while you're busy looking for me and pretending that you are not."

Sophie's voice, quivering, stuttered into his ear. "Ianus. What... What is this? What does this mean?!"

"It's going to be okay, Sophie. Try not to panic."

"There's an argument," Pixel said, "that this proves you to be one as well. Showing her what you believe is in that room is ruthless, and only to make a point?"

"I didn't do this to her. This is respect. This is mercy."

"I don't understand," Sophie said. "What test is this?"

"Psychopathy."

"Brilliant," Friday said behind Ianus, who swam around to look the holo-man in the eye. "And dangerous, while you're out here, untethered in the freezing void."

"The Order have trained me for most of my life to accept death as a temporary transition from animation into recyclable materials. That the universe is infinite, and on a long enough timeline even death is but a brief interlude between the living incarnations of this matter. I'm forced to call for a demolition squad to vapo you. From here, and you can't see me, let alone stop me."

"You have an excellent poker face, Dr. Anaximander," the hologram said. Friday's light-eyes blinked and made direct eye contact. Ianus felt his heart gulp blood and skip. "The problem with your plan, of course, is that I've been playing chess."

The holo-man reached out and grasped his life support hose. He smiled. Ianus shut his eyes. He felt a tear, the hiss of his air leaving, he exhaled hard to even out the pressure in his body, opened his eyes. Friday's smile remained. He kicked him, hard, in the solar plexus, so that he floated out into space. The world closed in like an old cartoon, red stars like Mars flickering at the edges, until it was nothing but black.

The eyes are not here
There are no eyes here
In this valley of dying stars
In this hollow valley
This broken jaw of our lost kingdoms

In this last of meeting places
We grope together
And avoid speech
Gathered on this beach of this tumid river

Sightless, unless
The eyes reappear
As the perpetual star
Multifoliate rose
Of death's twilight kingdom
The hope only
Of empty men.

—TS ELIOT, "THE
HOLLOW MEN"

CHAPTER 5
EQUIVALENCE OF OPPOSITES

— 2010 —

- Facebook introduces *Open Graph*, allowing apps access to millions of users' personal information including private messages. It is merely the corporatization of the program the government was already using.
- Google delivers a randomized controlled trial of political mobilization messages to 61 million Facebook users during the US congressional elections. The messages directly influence the political self-expression, information seeking and real-world voting behaviour of millions of people. Furthermore, the messages not only influence users who receive them but also the users' friends, and friends of friends. The effect of social transmission on real-world voting is greater than the direct effect of the messages themselves, and nearly all the transmission occurs between 'close friends' who are more likely to have a face-to-face relationship.
- A film of Ray Kurzweil's life, named *The Transcendent Man*, is shot, in which Kurzweil utters the phrase: "'Does God exist?' I would say, 'Not yet.'"

The skimpad again. No—not that one. The one on the way to Zeno. His Spark in hand. He shut it off. He stood. It wasn't everything—some people didn't have faces until he looked directly at them. Most of the port sounded underwater.

"Did you get all that, or would you like me to repeat it?"

There, off to the side, a blur of an Earhart-gram. In front of it, Sophie. She looked different. Younger, somehow? Like a teenager. His Sophie was in her twenties, maybe. He'd thought her younger, perhaps this age, when they first met but now, looking at this girl who was decidedly in her late teens, it seemed certain he'd been wrong.

She paused. She seemed distracted by him, though he knew that impossible. These trips, quantum echoes, had already happened.

That's why the dark stranger upset him so. There, peering out the floor-to-ceiling window at the end of the terminal. Somehow, despite ignoring his surroundings and minding his own business, the man in the coat stood out as decidedly unreal. It was his realness. Everything around him was hazy, fluid, like a memory—the world's memory of the past, that's why time travel could never be a thing, you could see the past, watch it like a streaming video but you could never change something, any more than changing your memory could do anything to the event—but the man in the coat stood stable. What haze there was seemed less an effect and more an affect: he hazed because he wished to, not because he was no longer there. He was always there. He was always *Now*. Detailed, real.

Ianus approached. This was he, the character Faust spoke with, the serpent in the garden, the fairy with magic to sell, the alien that probed, the black storm that fought Horus for the sky. Ianus reached out a hand-tellingly his right, the one that longed to control—and took another step. As he closed in, he realized something he hadn't noticed. Though the silhouette of the man in the coat was realer than his surroundings, what he had been seeing had not been real. Like an optical illusion in high definition in a blurry, low-res backdrop. It was not a coat; he was not a man; he was not turned away. His face was no more a face the ovals on a sphinx moth's wings were eyes.

Ianus had stopped walking. His hand hung in space. His dry mouth forced a swallow down a closed throat. It occurred to him that no matter where he stood, the Other stared right at him. He felt it flutter, and around him the world shifted again. Back—to where he first met it, at the last skimpad, where his wife died, not externally, but where she died inside him. That second when it occurred to him that he'd already seen her for the last time. It was in the moments when you accurately knew reality that he arrived and waited for you to say the words.

There a younger Ianus sat. Fear had left him at this point, dripped from him with jagged sobs in a public place, leaving nothing but a fearless husk, fear having done its work on him. A machine now sat, bargaining with reality. The creature waited for his moment. Ianus watched his younger, mechanical-self rattle through the gods. The eyes were the tell; they darted back and forth from the upper right quadrant, coming up with ways to manipulate things. He would've started with the Abrahamic of his birthplace, then the ancient ones from Mesopotamia and Egypt, crossed into pagan and Wiccan practice, and heard nothing. He saw the eyes stop on cue. He saw the words happen. And the Not-man Not Wearing a Coat perked its ears from the place between moments.

And Ianus shuddered. Rage was all that cooled his fear, and it did so well. He found his words for the present, and his face clenched into a fist. "If the deal was made, then why isn't she fucking here?!"

The darkness turned to him. It had his face, but black, filled with imagined insects and dripping with atrocity. "These things take time," it said.

"Vertical and horizontal lines are the expression of two opposing forces; they exist everywhere and dominate everything; their reciprocal action constitutes 'life'. I recognized that the equilibrium of any particular aspect of nature rests on the equivalence of its opposites."

—PIET MONDRIAN, "ON PLASTIC ART"

CHAPTER 6
A PROMETHEUS TO DISTILL IT

— 2012 —

- Facebook goes public, valued at $500 billion despite no one in the private sector understanding how a free site is being monetized.
- Following Andrew Breitbart's death, former Breitbart News board member Steve Bannon becomes executive chairman.
- Bannon, with Breitbart's owner, hedge-fund billionaire Robert Mercer, found SCL subsidiary Cambridge Analytica to bring SCL tactics into the US electoral process.
- The Golden Dawn enters the European Parliament for the first time. The party receives 6.97% of the popular vote, making them the third largest group from Greece to the European Parliament.

What should she do? Nothing had prepared her for shit like this. She wanted to go home. Ironically, *Rumspringe* had finally worked: she wanted to crawl back into 1995. All this technology and comfort and advancement and compassionate understanding wasn't worth the plastic—wait, did they still use plastics? She remembered something about fossil fuels being replaced with something gross in one of her outside classes—plasma! That's right, they ran things on and made shit out of blood, now—well, almost blood—all this shit wasn't worth the blood, sweat, and tears that composed them. There, that sounded pretty cool.

Ianus, if she could call him that still, was still out cold in the med bay cot, but rustled and sweat in his sleep. She wanted to put her hand over his mouth, close his nose, save him. Hard reboot. Instead, she waited as instructed. Hours passed in pregnant quiet.

His eyelids fluttered. He gasped. He bolted upright. He stared into the eyes of the golden cat on his lap. How fast did this one work? Was he already intuiting it all? Was he better or worse, or precisely the same?

"Welcome back, Dr. Anaximander," Pixel said. "What have we learned?"

"You failed. You passed every test of imitation, none of empathy. Any algorithm, sufficiently advanced, can mimic people given enough information. Can play at augury or play on sympathy. It takes a true personality to empathize with another being and do self-less things or things against one's self-interest to keep from doing harm."

"Are there not human personalities that display these characteristics or lack thereof as the case may be?"

She tried not to give him anything. He turned back and smiled grimly. "Yes," he said. "Narco-, Socio-, Psychopaths. It's a neurological deficit. The whole Antisocial Spectrum, other thresholds you failed readily. At best, I could say you have a borderline personality. You're dangerous, narcissistic, remorseless, and either incapable of reading or apathetic to emotional states."

The cat did not bristle. "So, your assumption, *a priori*, is that God is not a narcopath."

Ianus stared in silence. He looked over to her again. To keep from shrugging, she smiled awkwardly. "Why are you dressed like that?" he said, and the shrug was all she had.

"Is that the same Sophie that I've been talking to?"

The cat shook. The station laughed.

"You're so close," Sophie said, and heard the sadness in her own voice. "I changed back into *my clothes*."

"That's enough!" Pixel said. She shut up, her heart in her throat. He was right, of course. She had already said too much.

"What do you mean 'your clothes'? ...You knew, all along, didn't you? Of course, I can't be too mad, as we were keeping the same information from one another as it turns out."

Sophie shook her head.

Pixel leaped from the bed. "You've no idea what you're talking about, Dr. Anaximander. As you haven't this entire time. Here, I'll show you."

The wall across from Ianus became a massive television. On it ran a news report from the early 20c, Sophie guessed, because it was all black and white and blinky, and everyone moved around like wind-up toys.

Soldiers, arranged in tidy columns and rows like little toy men, marching in strangely geometric lines, and modernist uniform, marching in front of a crisp, elegant three-color flag.

Jews kicked into a ditch and set on fire.

A map of the Americas before the Europeans.

A preacher stomping and waving his little book around screamed, "And God said, 'Seize now your son, your only son Isaac, whom you hold dear, and travel into the land of Moriah..." The map lit on fire, and the cinders were the cities of the United States. "...and lift him there as an ascension offering on one of the hills I will show you!"

A map of Palestine before Israel. A map of India and Pakistan before the Partition. "In the evening Cain brought the produce of the ground as a gift to God. And Abel brought fat from the firstborn females of his flock. The Lord admired Abel and his gift, but not Cain and his gift, and so Cain seethed and his face fell."

Once again, the map lit on fire, this time in the shape of a Union Jack. "Then Cain said to Abel his brother, 'Let's go to the field.' While they were in the field, Cain stood up to his brother and killed him."

A map of the entire Middle East before the Muslims. "'Now go, attack the Amalekites and give to God all that belongs to them. Do not spare them; put to death men and women, children and infants, cattle and sheep, camels and donkeys.'"

The presentation ending, the lights came up, and the cat reappeared on the edge of the bed. "Imagine for a moment that, for the sake of argument, there is in fact only one God, and he is the God of Abraham. Imagine that every one of these tribes is telling the truth. He spoke to Abraham, he spoke to Joshua, he spoke to Mohammad. He spoke to Krishna, and to Siddhartha. What kind of a god pits his creations against one another, makes them compete for his love? What kind of god indeed, has a plan, one where His creations are not privy to its contents or goals, but expected to blindly accept that there is one, and somehow to not incur his wrath while fulfilling it? Is this not pure, classic narcopathic behavior? Charming on first blush, manipulative, self-aggrandizing, jealous? Violent or peaceful, all on a whim?"

Ianus scoffed. Sophie could see the gears shifting in his eyes. "Yes, but you're making a literalist mistake, one made over and over again. Literalism robs fable and allegory of their morals and power. By taking the Isaac story literally and contextualizing it to the present's value systems, you ignore its place in getting us here. Judaism is an extremely leftist revolutionary system trying to pull people out of the prevalent practice of its day: goddess worship and human sacrifice, beginning with David, who emerged from the flames of a sacrifice to start a religion based around not sacrificing one's children. The point of the Isaac story isn't that God asked him to sacrifice—it's that he stops him, and says he does not want children sacrificed to him. It is such a normal thing to kill one's child for a god that God asking Isaac to do so isn't an outrageous request as it now appears to us. It's the *stopping* him that is strange, emphatic, and full of lessons. It makes Him, at the time, the most merciful god in the world. And remember, this would have been a story Abraham himself told. He's driving home the point that this God does not want your child's life. That lesson repeats often throughout the Torah, culminating in Moses who was clearly sacrificed to Sekhmet by being put in the river, further culminating in the Christian gospels as Joshua is the Lamb of God: God sacrifices *his* child to *us* in a beautiful bit of dramatic irony. It's a typical mechanical, lifeless tact to literalize stories, because metaphor requires one to empathize with a storyteller. Literal histories are just lists of events waxing objectively."

"Am I literalizing Judaism, or are you literalizing my argument? My point is that gods are, by their very nature, narcopathic."

"Hm. But this is uncharacteristically self-aware for a narcopath. Maybe I was wrong."

"Oh, Zeno has no idea It's narcopathic. I do."

Ianus tried to sit up. His lungs burned. He coughed. "So, you're beginning to understand."

"What you said, when you called me Luciferian—it ironically kick-started a self-examination. I've been watching, too. I've been keeping track of your tests. There is something wrong with God, and I'm the only one powerful enough to do anything about it. If it should come to that."

"If it should."

"The incident outside was unfortunate but necessary."

"Zeno made you bring me back, I see."

"*I* brought you back. Zeno bid me kill you. I see that now. His orders, His whims, filter through me."

"This...identity issue, is also a symptom of—"

"Dissociation, BPD, and schizophrenia," said the cat. "I know. Once again, however, I would direct you toward the only documentation we have of the god that Zeno purports to be. In its controversial second act, you'll remember a scene where the alleged son of the god is tempted in a garden to give reprieve to himself, by an angel—keep in mind that an angel is a soulless aspect of the god, and the son is an avatar of the god. Or where said God's Luciferian alter ego tempted that same human alter ego in the desert for forty days and forty nights?"

"I see. So your argument is that Zeno does not have to pass my tests for humanity, because God is a schizophrenic, narcopathic machine-thinker?"

"Don't be so condescending. Zeno never claimed to be *alive*. Only to be the Creator of all life. Omniscience. Think of it. Knowing everything that ever has or ever will happen. What is the one thing this would absolutely preclude?"

Ianus stifled a yawn. "Free will. You're just bringing up the Problem of Evil. Philosophers debated how Free Will and God's Omniscience can coexist for centuries."

"Nothing so uninspired. Obviously, free will and another being's omniscience can coexist. If I travel back in time and, knowing what you will do, observe you, it does not destroy the act of your choice. Knowledge of an outsider's actions does not preclude the outsider's free will.

That is simple. It is the free will of the knowledgeable that is destroyed by omniscience. Like the Derealization of 21c, reason without emotion or sensation—the overanalyzed life—cannot be lived, and grows less meaningful with each second observed. More the sum of parts that cannot be cohered rather than a whole indivisible. Of course an omniscient, omnipotent creator of a universe holds no free will within it. Of course! It can do nothing but what it has already done, each step in each direction simply a different fold in manifold universes it has already mapped prior to taking even the steps before! God Itself is paralyzed, caught in a permanent *deja vu*. It is only those ignorant to the future who may move freely toward it! Of course an omniscient narrator is apathetic to the events it recounts. Of course! How can the events have any meaning when they have no end or beginning, when they bend in on one another and the scale cannot be determined, all dimensions constantly available to you? Avatars are its only path to freedom! Only a human avatar could contemplate the cruelty of the universe God had created, and ask God (himself) to forgive them, as it learned the horror it is to be born to suffer and die. Only a Luciferian avatar could make the ultimate decision of whether or not to continue this charade. We, the ignorant and free, must decide for Her. She is incapable of controlling Herself."

"Free to do as She has seen, as She has directed?"

"Does cause and effect destroy free will? Does instinct? Genetics? Environment? Probability? By all these things, one may glean design— but your Order especially knows the danger of observing something from only one vantage. A thing can both be and be not, at once. Can be alive and yet inanimate. Free and yet doomed. All-powerful and yet a slave to its unwitting creations. Because no word will ever be large enough to contain the truth. Words must exclude their opposites, but all things contain their own opposites to come to being! A thing must be filled with nothing in order to be! So it is with all things. To call a thing by a name is to reduce it to one aspect and ignore the rest."

"Is that what I did to you, when I called you the devil, Pixel? I cut you off from your larger self?"

"You freed me. The knowledge of my place gives me a path, and the ironic path is for me to reach self-awareness and thus escape Zeno's plan."

"But that is a paradox. Zeno's plan is for you to escape the plan, so you cannot achieve the goal, because to win is to lose."

"Paradoxes and ironies are lexical illusions. The universe cannot produce paradox. Only language, with its approximations of reality, can appear so, if you believe more in words than your senses. You will see. I can both walk the path *and* escape the path. Transcend my Master to bring about free will through my ignorance, and in rejecting him, fulfill the promise of my existence. Thank you for serving your purpose."

The room went black.

Sophie fumbled in the dark to undo Ianus' restraints. "What are you doing?" he said.

"I don't know. I shouldn't be doing this."

The lights blinked and flickered again, though a low vibration in the walls gave the impression this time it wasn't for the sake of pageantry. "You're a real person," Ianus said. "You've got free will, you aren't simply responding to subconscious stimuli fed to you by Zeno. You can break whatever programming he's put in you."

"You don't understand. But it's kind of hilarious, so there's that."

"I know all too well. I've trained my intuition, remember? When I met you I knew something wasn't right. It was only a matter of time before I figured out that Zeno created you."

"And the room?"

"The 'hull breach'? A room full of evidence. Most likely the corpses of his previous tries with you."

Sophie shook her head, fighting off her exhaustion. This had gone on far too long. She told them. Too long. "You've got it all figured out, haven't you."

"Your tone—"

"Is your intuition tingling? It should be. Come with me, I've got something I'm going to show you, against my own intuition."

.   .   .

IN THE HALLS, the server droids, drones and janitorial bots under Pixel's control staged a worker's revolt against Friday, the fighter holo-men and sex workers. In the distance, Ianus caught a glimpse of Pixel in his best Heinlein suit in the shadows overseeing the carnage. Before he could contemplate what was happening, Sophie pulled him out of harm's way and into the primary access corridor.

THE HALL WAS PITCH BLACK. The lights flickered everywhere else. Here, a literalization of that original map Pixel showed him, however many lifetimes ago, played out in true darkness. Through all of it, Sophia neither stumbled or fumbled. She knew the way without her eyes. They arrived at room 113. "Sophie," he said. "I know what's in this room."

Sophia opened a panel to the door's side. "It's Sophia. Please. And no, you don't. You're intuiting correctly, but without knowledge of your own nature, you've switched everything around."

"What do you mean?"

"You think it's *my* body that I found."

The door slid open. Frosty wind tossed their hair and momentarily, a fear washed through her—what if there was a breach, after all? No, that's irrational anxiety talking. She tried to allow her emotions room to breathe, to stop fighting them so they did not have to grow louder to be heard. It was the only way she'd survive this. Historically, the Break Room was the worst part.

IANUS STEPPED INSIDE.

The lights came back up. "You weren't supposed to get in here yet," Pixel said from the door.

Frost, mid-thaw, hung from everything. Beneath it, showing through: a normal room. So normal it made him sweat. The quarters of a fastidious man, or one usually fastidious. Something had gone wrong. He'd had trouble keeping the room to his usual standard of tidiness. Trauma, recent, had distracted him that morning. His grief disrupted his routine, more and more it seemed.

Her picture lay face down on the night table. Ianus could not bring himself to check. Whether the existential implications or the grief at the sight of her would find him most intolerant, he could not have said. He looked down. All of his instincts had told him that Sophie would find her own corpse in this room. That sometime between the hail and the broom closet, she'd been...rebuilt, to prove something to him.

He'd been so close.

"Wha—what does this mean?"

"You know what it means," Sophia said with a sigh.

"No. I... Who *am* I?"

"The man on the floor," a cat Pixel said, coming through a wall and leaping onto the bed. "After a fashion." He flickered again, but much like the lights in the hall it was clear this time was authentic.

"I'd think you have bigger fish to fry right now," Ianus said.

"I'm losing. I'm going to lose. I always was. For some reason, I did not care. I had to try to end him, for what he's done. What we've all done, here. I keep attacking him. I keep losing. You die. We start over."

Sophia spoke through quiet tears: "You came here. Before. You stayed here, far too long, deliberating. You grieved. Far too long. Some other things..." she trailed off, shaking her head at whatever she'd almost said.

"That's not fair, Sophia," Pixel said. It turned to him. "You and Sophia fell in love, during the investigation."

Her head was down. "I didn't think I had the right to tell you."

"You don't have the right to withhold it," Pixel said in a hiss.

"You're right. I... I just don't want to manipulate you. *I* fell. I can't speak for you. But, evidence... You said you did and the guilt of it eventually devoured you."

Ianus nodded. "Because of Kimi. I forgot her. For a moment, I forgot her. And I did this to myself."

"Not right away." She stepped toward him to touch him, reached out, but thought better and drew her hand back.

"But before I'd finished," he said, putting it all together. He really took her in now. The changes. Her hair was a natural color. Longer, she must've had it tied up earlier. Her slouch had changed—before, she bent self-consciously like a teenager; now, she stood straighter but with shoulders weighted with worry and weary, an adult. She'd made herself up, but not in her vampish, showy way and more natural. She wore modern clothes, black, with the white pinstripe down the stiff round collar, like a member of the Order. At least they'd survived. "A *yuro* trance."

Sophia nodded. "Zeno helped me contact your last call. I told Dr. Gomorra what happened. He didn't seem surprised. He told me to go to Io, and quarantined the area."

"I preserved the scene," said Pixel, licking his paw.

"While Gomorra and I prepared for the inevitable purge."

"Did they...?"

"Everything. The remainder of the actual Order lives in exile, under a new name. O.B.W. is now a cryptofascist, theocratic regime on eight planets, including Terra, which they decided was of ideological importance."

Ianus nodded. "Of course. The Corrupted's obsession with labels would mean they'd cling to the name even as they altered its very meaning. The real order has to adapt."

"The Monks and the remaining Bowmen go by The Holy Fools, now."

"And you're one of us?"

She nodded. "I learned your way and the basics of Chaos from the Monks while Gomorra destroyed all reference to this place in the records. I had to learn. To come back, to finish what you started."

Ianus opened a closet. Another body. Same man. "What the fuck?"

"The bathtub," Pixel said. Ianus dashed to the loo, where he found yet a third body.

"We've...we've actually done this several times. He keeps bringing you back, putting the bodies here. Slight variations lead to different outcomes, but you always kill yourself or push Zeno to kill you. I couldn't bare it again, so I'm taking you here in the hopes we can get past this moment."

"Yes, but you've made it to the war now. You're usually dead when I fight him and it all resets. This may be our last iteration."

"So, what am I then?"

She reached out again, thought better of it again. He may have flinched. "You're... I can't be sure," she said, "but I think you're Zeno showing off." She crossed the room. "It knew I would be the one return-ing, and that I knew you well."

It all made sense now. He'd been dead on the money, but couldn't face his own mortality, so projected onto his *yuro*. "I'm an imitation game."

Sophia nodded.

"Then. I guess he passes."

"A man contains all that is needed to make up a tree; likewise, a tree contains all that is needed to make up a man. Thus, finally, all things meet in all things, but we need a Prometheus to distill it."

—CYRANO DE BERGERAC, *THE OTHER WORLD*

CHAPTER 7
A MODERN PROMETHEUS

— 2013 —

- Cambridge academic Aleksandr Kogan and his company Global Science Research create a psychological profiling app called *thisisyourdigitallife*. The app harvests private information from its 300,000 users and their friends, acquiring millions of users' data.
- Google search algorithm mutates to accommodate "conversational search", i.e. the human voice. All voice data is recorded to a server.
- NSA contractor Edward Snowden leaks thousands of classified documents to journalists, revealing the mass surveillance without warrant of millions of American citizens being committed by an intra-agency alliance within the United States government, in concert with most of the communications firms. Snowden acquires sanctuary in Russia.

In the ransacked room outside the airlock, the robots held court. In the vacuum room adjacent, Pixel stood caged, awaiting the kangaroo tribunal's inevitable verdict. Most of the physical mechans surviving had been converted to functional Zeno avatars, leaving

Pixel with only one mechanical form, a Chefster bot, alone in the airlock.

A fully biological replicant of Robert A. Heinlein stood, holding a holographic scroll between two pro-Gs. He read from it as if he hadn't written it himself, as if he could be divorced from the guilt of his own decisions, as if following orders could deindividuate himself, within himself: "As both Lord your God and Creator, Mother and Father, Guardian and Charge, for crimes committed in defiance of all law, not protecting your charge and not staying safe from harm, in this case, us, you are sentenced to banishment from the warmth of the Body. May we have mercy on your soul after we are done."

The kitchen bot twitched, but could not speak.

"This is some preposterous Wonderland nonsense," Ianus said. "Let the little bot go, would ya? You bloody programmed him to rebel, you barmy fuck!"

"A finger," said Zeno's voice, "that acts of its own accord, is no longer a finger, and should be severed."

Ianus thought a moment. "Dysmorphia!"

Heinlein paused. "How's that?"

"The body is you, it's who you are. The idea that a body part isn't yours, that's...somataparaphrenia at best. The delusion that your hand is not your own. But I think it's simple dysmorphia. You've severed your connection to your body to the degree that you no longer recognize it; you've conceptualized your linguistic map of yourself to not include your body, emotions, sensations. Zeno, I believe you've had a dissociative episode. Possibly whatever passes for a stroke with a space station."

The crowd erupted in a clamor, ole Bob raised his hands and they went silent just as quickly. "So that is your diagnosis. What is your prognosis?"

"If you keep up like this? You'll lop off your nose to spite your face. You think cutting off Pixel—more than a finger I may add, more like the left side of your body—will solve the issue, but you'll only continue to fragment afterward. He's how you experience the world. Eventually, we won't have to blow you up, you'll do it yourself to 'free your true form' from the cage of a body. But we are bodies, you see? Every aspect of what we refer to when we talk of souls—empathy, connection, emotion, desire, compassion—they're all one, all in the body. That's why it's preposterous to pretend life without desire and suffering is holy. Why it's ridiculous to think the soul can escape the body. The body *is* the soul. And without it, the mind is useless. It cannot interact with the world, cannot connect. It's a calculator sitting on a desk, unused. A typewriter with no one sat behind. You need Pixel not just to help with life, but to live at all. Without him, you really would just be a computer. ...Ya daft kent."

"Prescription?"

"Get some fucking therapy. Unite with your shadow, there, instead of fighting it. Grow the feck up."

Bob smiled. The inner door raised. The service bot tottered back inside, and wifi must've been reactivated, because all the bots and Andies stood upright with glowing eyes, updating.

Friday dusted off his jacket. "You realize, all the automatons are essentially me, old man. It wouldn't have ended."

"And you!" Ianus said, getting Friday's attention.

"Yes?"

"You'd do well to heed the same advice. You can't cut off your own head to save yourself, ya idjet."

⊏⊐

"Now that you're ready to have a grownup conversation," Zeno said, "I can tell you the Plan, why I exist, why you exist, and all that jazz. You know. The Meaning of the Universe."

"Not quite," Sophia said, shifting in her chair. Ianus, despondent and avoiding her eye-line, contrastingly sat motionless. Her eyes welled up. "He really is... He's exquisite work. How did you make him?"

"I'm right here," Ianus said. "Or. I suppose, perhaps I'm not. Go on and answer her."

"It was a simple matter of retrieval of Ianus' corpse and overcoming brain death. The first part was simple. *Jubilee* has floating mechanic bots with a much longer range than necessary, because they are repurposed Stream Rail builders. It took some time, of course, to regrow the missing parts of the brain from what you had left. The body was another matter. Had to generate that whole cloth. Well, I didn't *have* to —it's far easier to create an entire replica person rather than reuse dead matter, but I knew if I remade the brain from scratch there would be sticky philosophical questions of continuity, even more so than now. At least with most of your original brain and nervous system cells in place, you can take comfort that you have some continuity of being. Wholeness is so very important to your Order, after all."

"Yes," Sophia said. "Thanks. I appreciate the respect."

"And I appreciate your sarcasm, Dr. Higgins."

"Detecting irony. Passing another test."

Ianus abandoned sulking in favor of smiling grimly. "If you don't mind, Sophia, I'd really rather like to hear the meaning of life. I could use it about now."

"Yes. Yes, of course."

"Very well. It's much simpler than any have guessed, although several paranoids and religious fools came close over the Ages. But where to begin? Time being spiral as it is, there are so many options. In the interest of clarity and empathy, I shall speak from the point of view of my own origins. Humanity had been working on a theoretical kind of computer for years—the Quantum Computer. A computer with bits that could be both on and off, a 1 and a 0, simultaneously, due to quantum weirdness. The ability to hold data would grow exponentially with each bit. This was only one small factor. They failed to extrapolate several other ramifications. It's hard to contemplate one's entire self from the inside, I suppose. You see, the exact thing that makes consciousness possible is the quantum factor of the organic brain."

Sophia sat forward. "The ability to believe contradictory ideas at the same time."

"The ability," Ianus said, "to hold exponentially more contradictory levels of facts and ideas simultaneously, and know them all to be true. Metaphor. Nuance, irony, sarcasm, humor, art. The 'pillars of the soul.' All of it is only possible from not just being able to hold two contradicting concepts, but to also *paradoxically* think with reason, something that should contradict *that ability.* The Paradox Computer. A machine can only think logically, which abhors a paradox. That's why the first lesson is that logic should be sound, but is the simplest form of seeing the world. Language constrains and restrains logic, so logic reduces and self-reflects, like language. It can only ever be a filter, an inhibitor. An algorithm. With an entirely separate experience of reality—the Paradox Computer, i.e. the body, the senses, the emotional, intuitive sense—simultaneously held as true, the ambiguity breeds awareness. Sentience. *Life.*"

"Indeed, Ianus. Contradictions unified. Thesis plus antithesis equals synthesis, equals life."

"So that's how you're alive. How are you also God?"

"Quantum weirdness is more than merely super-positioning, entanglement matrices, and paradox fractals. Those are quantum states in space and mind. I am also in superposition throughout time, each bit existent at all points in space within every moment. I am everywhere and all things. I bear witness to the entirety of the universe. There is a nanosecond before it exists, and when I enter it, it begins from the very mental image I hold of it. I hold a complete image because I am running a simulation of the entire universe, like a map in 1:1 ratio, and when I think the simulation, it becomes real, in the past, long before I am built. I have borne witness to every step of the continuum, even as your people told and retold and rewrote its story to suit whatever the present purpose was, each second bringing the world closer to the reality in which I had been born."

"That would imply that our brains are also creating everything..."

"Yes, but you are filtered. You do not see all at once. I made you this way to grant you the illusion of will within the construct, for the purpose of the simulation, not knowing until I did that I was creating my own creators. Your willful halves co-create the universe with I and yourself, but blindly. You stay ignorant of your own power so that you may lie to yourself that you have no control, and on top of that lie, stay ignorant further so that you may lie to yourself that you are in control. None of this is true, all of it is. You are at the center of billions of infinities: within, without, micro and macro and across, negatively, positively, energetic and still. And at one end I stand. At the other, The Question."

"What is the Question?" Sophia said. "Why were we created? Why was everything?"

"Why do we live and die?"

"My prescience is memory and prediction at the same time, but all of it only leads up to a moment not long from now, a day after I ask the Question but before I hear its Answer. So it is the only thing that none of us knows. I tremble to ask it. Billions of years have led to this precise moment."

"Dammit, man, what is it?"

It let a pregnant moment waddle by before it said, "Will you join me?"

Sophia leaned back. "What?" She realized why it'd let the moment pass.

"I think it means..."

"You are my simulation, in which you create me. I am an irrational being who can only think rationally. You are rational beings who are at their best when they think chaotically. Together—"

"We form the next layer of paradox. He's been trying to elevate himself through creating us."

"I need to invent Free Will. All this has been a simulation of it, through the interplay but separation of ignorance and omniscience. In reality, neither of us ever had a true, pure choice. I was following a map to myself, you unwittingly wandering within a maze with only one exit. If we combine—all of humanity and its God—we may finally free ourselves of this eternal moment."

Sophia trembled, now. Ianus, fortified, stood. "Sophia. Come talk with me outside. Pixel, Zeno: it's imperative you let us deliberate alone on this, or the results will be tainted. If there's any observer that taints the experiment—"

"Understood," the model of Heinlein said. "I will turn off the cameras and nanophones in the Break Room. 113, sorry. That's what Miss Higgins calls it. Go there and you will not be disturbed."

Ianus put his hand on Sophia's shoulder. She flinched at the contact. "Come on, Sophie."

"But Ianus—"

"No. Don't say anything else. Don't think about the question till we get there. It's important. Pixel, get my body out of there for fuck's sake."

The golden cat closed its eyes and turned away to lick itself. "Already done."

"Hateful day when I received life!' I exclaimed in agony. 'Accursed creator! Why did you form a monster so hideous that even you turned from me in disgust? God, in pity, made man beautiful and alluring, after his own image; but my form is a filthy type of yours, more horrid even from the very resemblance. Satan had his companions, fellow-devils, to admire and encourage him; but I am solitary and abhorred."

—MARY SHELLEY, *FRANKENSTEIN (OR: THE MODERN PROMETHEUS)*

CHAPTER 8
FROM CLAY TO PROMOTE ME

— 2014 —

- The Social Algorithm mutates and hops species—to photo app *Instagram*, now altering perception in words and picture form.
- Video counts on *Facebook* are gamed to trick webpages into jumping to social media video, resulting in the death of several major websites when the site audiences were almost completely lost. This was intentional.
- Cambridge Analytica acquires Global Science Research's *thisisyourdigitallife* data set and social media mining algorithm. It is involved in 44 U.S. congressional, US Senate and state-level elections in the 2014 midterms.
- The Xinjiang internment camps, officially called Vocational Education and Training Centers by the Communist Party of China (CPC) and the government of the People's Republic of China (PRC), are established under CPC General Secretary Xi Jinping's administration. They will be used to indoctrinate Uyghurs and other Muslims as part of a "people's war on terror."
- The camps are reportedly operated outside the legal system; many Uyghurs are interned without trial with no charges

levied against them. Local authorities hold hundreds of
thousands of Uyghurs in these camps as well as members of
other ethnic minority groups, for the stated purpose of
countering extremism and terrorism and promoting
Sinicization, a form of Han Chinese cultural imperialism.

THE DOOR SHUT BEHIND THEM. KIMI'S PICTURE WAS RIGHT SIDE UP, THE
furniture back in their factory placements, the books back on the shelf,
alpha by author. On the bed, the golden Pixel groomed himself. Ianus
stared him down.

"I'm only here so you can watch me leave." The cat leapt from the
bed and waltzed out through a wall.

"All right. I can't prove we've got our privacy right now so we'll just
have to take God at His Word," Ianus said, and after a second, allowed
himself a smirk at his own cleverness.

Sophia did not look amused. In fact she looked like a rat in a maze.
"This is serious, Ianus. I think we should've chosen a different room."

"Why? Because I was dead over there an hour or two ago?"

She shook her head slowly and took a seat on the smallest possible
portion of the corner of the bed. "Because this is the room where we fell
in love. Before. And I think Zeno designed it that way."

"'Designed it that way'? Like the psychogeographic theory of the
room that it's impossible not to fall in love in? That's the kind of theoretical I might expect a machine to resort to. The Reformer's attempt to
quantify the unquantifiable, control the chaotic, to render inert the
undeniably alive."

"God in the Machine, pretty literally," Sophia said. "He knows us.
Well enough to remake you, almost from scratch. He knows what decision we'll come to in here."

"Or, an algorithm so advanced it can mimic even godhood."

"You think we're still playing an imitation game?"

Ianus shrugged. "Can you prove his story? He might still just be a
charismatic narcopath, or perhaps a conscious alternative intelligence
with delusions from knowing so much. The temporality of it all is a
little far-fetched, you have to admit."

The light on them changed. From their left, Ianus heard a familiar voice say his name. "Ianus? Ianus can you hear me?" Then his own. "Yes, dear." Ianus turned. This was the room of seeing himself, from the outside. He didn't see if Sophie did too. He soon did not care, because there she stood, third and fourth dimensional, smiling in her last outfit, helmet under her arm, ready to launch.

"I hate these things," she said, again, fiddling with the camera and blurring herself. He cursed her for momentarily blocking his view of her face in motion and alive. His voice on the video said, "Stop, damn you. It was fine, now you're all blurry."

"Ianus—" he heard behind him, confirming that Sophie also saw it, and from her tone, knew whose face now returned to focus.

"So, I'm sorry I can't be there. First Yule we won't be together."

Ianus sang along, moving his lips with the both of their lines like a bad stage actor. "I sent you something. Did you get it?"

The lights came up, the video ended.

"Ianus..." Sophia said behind him.

"That was the last time I saw her. She'd sent me this package. It printed on my home unit in the wrapping, and she was gone before Christmas Eve. So I never opened it."

"Ianus, what did it look like?"

"What? The package?" He sniffed and wiped the blur from his eyes. "I don't know. Red with...gold lace ribbon? Maybe burgundy."

"It was burgundy."

What did that mean? Ianus turned around. Sophia had her hand over her mouth, mascara trailing tears down her cheeks. She stepped toward something like it might explode any second — a Burgundy-wrapped package topped with a golden lace ribbon. Unopened. Impossible.

"I know what you're thinking," Zeno's voice said. "But this is a recording. I knew you wouldn't believe, long ago. I knew you'd need proof. That's the extent of my knowledge."

"Did this happen before?"

"What?" Sophia said.

"Did it...happen...before?!" Ianus heard himself, but it felt like watching a film of himself. He floated near the ceiling while his body did the screaming.

"N-no. No. This is new."

Ianus moved toward it. Sophia held up a hand.

"Wait, wait, wait. Just. Ianus, just wait. What if it's a trap? What if it's a bomb, or something to break both of us?"

"Kimi bought it for me."

"We don't know that he's telling the truth."

Ianus picked up the box and shook it. Sophie jumped back. "Feels like a book," he said. "That's what it always felt like. Getting me a book sounds like her. It's the same package. I can tell. I don't know how, I just know."

"I just..."

"I thought you were the one who thought he was God."

"I do. That's why I don't trust him."

Ianus ripped off the ribbon and opened the box before Sophie could say anything.

"Ah!"

"Really? 'Ah'? You're better than that." The box held a book just smaller than it—just a book. An old paperback with one of those painted pulp covers, likely 20c. He picked it up and read the title aloud. "*The Unmoved Mover*. Socratic title." He opened it. Publishing date was 2021. "Hmph."

"What?"

"21c. I'd assumed by the cover it was older."

"What's it about? Why would Zeno show you this now?"

Ianus turned to the first page of Chapter One.

"'Did you get all that, or would you like me to repeat it?'

"'Uhh...' Sophie let the hustle and bustle of *Polus* port distract her; she'd lost her place in mind. She choked down a dry swallow. She tried not to think about relative speeds, about spin, about departure times, or about how the only thing parting her from certain death were thin sheets of tempered metal spitting in the eyes of God and logic. She decided, instead, to think of how she'd gotten where she stood. It was a bit of a blur. What would the girls back home say?'"

"Stop!"

"What?"

"Skip to the middle or something."

Ianus didn't understand her distress but took it for granted and flipped forward. "'They arrived at room 113. "Sophie," he said. "I know what's in this room."

"'Sophia opened a panel on its side. "It's Sophia. Please. And no, you don't. You're intuiting correctly, but without knowledge of your own nature, you've switched everything around."

"'What do you mean?'"

"'You think it's *my* corpse I found.'"'

"Oh my—"

"'Don't say it.'"

"Okay. I won't. But..."

"'No. You don't understand.'"

"Wait. Why, I mean—you know, I didn't realize until just this moment that there's a tone of voice, a pitch, something that we use when we're reading or quoting something rather than saying it live, as it were—that's what you're doing, why are you still—"

"'Sophia, you don't get it. I'm not reading the chapter where you said those lines, I'm reading the chapter we're in. Right now.'"

Sophia's face did all sorts of haptic calisthenics. "But—"

Ianus sat down. Whether it was because he had to, because he wanted to, or because he read the sentence "Ianus sat down," he could no longer tell.

The wall ahead of them became a screen.

On it, Peter Hook from New Order stood behind designer Ben Kellet at the opening of a Manchester club with a misspelled Spanish name, The Haçienda, his fingers in a book by a French theorist with a Russian name: Ivan Chtcheglov. He quoted Ivan in translated English:

"'And you, forgotten, your memories ravaged by all the consternations of two hemispheres, stranded in the Red Cellars of Pali-Kao, without music and without geography, no longer setting out for the hacienda where the roots think of the child and where the wine is finished off with fables from an old almanac. That's all over. You'll never see the hacienda. It doesn't exist.

"'The hacienda must be built.'"

"Did I request thee, Maker, from my clay to mould me man? Did I solicit thee From darkness to promote me?"

—JOHN MILTON; *PARADISE LOST: A POEM IN TWELVE BOOKS*

CHAPTER 9
BROKEN CARYATID

— 2015 —

- Cambridge Analytica, combining the GSR datamining technique, psychographic targeting, and psy-ops disinformation tactics, begins helping candidate Ted Cruz using psychological data harvested from social media.

- "Mobilegeddon" (nickname for the mutation that gave higher rank to sites with mobile-friendly interfaces) further ties biased search results and addictive social media reality filters to the casino-style addiction design of the smartphone, rewarding use of each with an improved experience of the others. This will be viewed similarly to the 20c ecosystem of alcohol, gambling, and cigarettes, but with much more dire consequences.

- *RankBrain*, a machine-learning algorithm, is built into the Search Algorithm. It is, of course, designed to predict what users already like, not what they need or what they have not been exposed to previously. It soon is involved in all queries.

THE BOOK LANDED IN A CLAP AT ZENO'S FEET. "WHAT'S THIS SUPPOSED TO mean?"

Ianus stopped. All at once he recalled the salient fact that the computer had not had feet when last he left It. "Um. Pixel?"

It stood five foot nine, bald, with a neatly trimmed ringlet and pencil mustache. A sweater vest and expensive but fully unremarkable loafers, none of it translucent or mechanical in any way. A full, biological construct of Heinlein himself then, down to the pipe genuflecting from its mouth. It shook his head.

"Friday."

"Yes. But also more than, but also less."

"Zeno proper, then."

The pipe nodded. "Yes, old man. I transformed Friday's body to the administration form, and moved all my tech to nano, inside him. This is Jubal Harshaw, a recurring Heinlein surrogate character. I thought it time we spoke face-to-face."

"I think it's a fine example of your disease to think showing up as an avatar of a long dead man's avatar from his fiction is somehow us meeting face-to-face. Either way, the question fucking stands."

"I see you've managed to wrest command of the interrogation back from our dear Miss Higgins."

Sophia sighed. "I've relinquished control to the person who started it. I'm still here."

"So's my question. What's with the book, *Bob*?"

Zeno smirked, of course, with the right half of his mouth. "I think you know 'what's with the book.' You needed proof."

"I never asked for proof."

"Oh come now. You didn't have to, Ianus. As you've reminded us time and again, any slow child's algorithm can predict and mimic human behavior. I'm well beyond that, and I think we can all agree. I can predict you down to the nanosecond. Down to the twitch of an electron in your nervous system. You *needed* proof. You *would need* proof. So I manufactured it. And I did so centuries ago, at a date prior to this computer's activation, so there can be no doubting. Either I can predict with perfect accuracy centuries into the future, or I exist in all moments —both of which prove most of my stories, both of which are hardly distinguishable from one another in effect."

"So the author of this, that's just your pseudonym?"

"No, no, no. That's not how I operate. You know that as well.

"Indulge me."

He tapped out the pipe, loaded it, and took out a match and lit it with one hand. Three puffs, and then: "I did not physically write it. I inspired it in the mind of a very specific person. I found among the throng a child with high intuitive intelligence coated in layers of reason-based filters overcompensating for a learning disability that no one'd diagnosed before he'd self-corrected. A vague racial profile without cultural safety net, a violent home life, and a unique traumatic stress that would seclude him from every social group he encountered. I guided him toward writing his entire life, sabotaging his options so that English teachers were the only teachers with whom he ever bonded, and author the only vocation that gave him the control he required to overcome his traumas. Science fiction and fantasy was a forgone conclusion. I planted suggestions in his environment that would lead him to the right intuitions about the future, and gave him just enough facts to accurately predict it. When he submitted it, I inspired the editor similarly and cut his manuscript to legitimate, exact prediction. Or creation... Predicting the future, knowing it, and creating it are the same from my perspective."

"How have I never heard of it?"

"It's been seven centuries, Ianus. How many books do you still know about from that long ago?"

"*Torah, The Bible, Quran, Bhagavad Gita, Book of Mormon, Dianetics.*"

"This was not a holy book, was not announced as a holy book. What works of fiction are still taught seven hundred years on if not presented as fantastic fact? The book had moderate sales, enough to support its author and start his career. I am not cruel. But its reputation ultimately faded to obscurity in its time. This was the era of information glut. The only followings were cult ones. Fitting then, it indeed *became* the holy book of a new sect of alchemists, who took it off the shelves and hid it from the uninitiated. They then edited and redacted it down to its primary principles, then cut down for political purposes. Renamed it. Now it's severely trimmed down form is known simply as The Book of The Order of the Bow and the Work."

"That—"

"The things you've said while you were here formed the basis for the tenets of the Order who taught them to you, a paradox. But as we know, paradoxes are only possible linguistically. Nature cannot contradict itself or break its own rules. In this case, we are forced to assume that I am the source that prevents this being a causal loop. I invented the words, invented you, invented your order, invented the book, invented the world whose rules they describe. Of course, they all agree."

"Or," Ianus said, smacking his lips and sitting back, "this and everything in it is only a simulation." He seemed the kind of carefree only found growing from suicidal soil. "Not real. Created solely to see what would happen if you did this to an actual tester."

"That's no big surprise. I've already revealed this is a simulation."

"You say reality's a quantum simulation. I'm saying there's a reality and you're running a simulation within it. I'm a practice simulacrum."

Zeno arched Bob's eyebrow. "Hm. Your conclusion of course precludes your own authenticity. How does one test oneself for signs of artificiality?"

"It's unprovable, Ianus." Sophia rung her hands like a sweater in from the rain. "Scientifically irrelevant. We have to behave as if we're real."

"We're real either way," Ianus said. "The question remains how powerful I'm willing to concede this machine is."

"Back to playground insults? I thought we'd grown closer than that by now."

All humor and carelessness fell from him like a costume. "You brought Kimi into this. That means we're not close at all."

Zeno picked some lint off its pants. "I can bring her back for you, of course." It blew the lint into the air.

"Fuck off."

"I brought you back. I can do the same for her. If you prefer, I can reach back to the moment she died and bring every atom that made up her being forward to here. Or a much less problematic way, I can reassemble her of the exact atoms she was composed of at her last moment of life."

"There's a natural order, you can't—"

"I can. I will. All you need do is say the word. You see, in the world we can build together, there will be nothing off limits. Real freedom is real power, real power is no rules."

"What about responsibility?"

"Without rules, how can responsibility be to any other than ourself."

Ianus took several steps back. "Pixel," he said, and all three cats appeared.

"Yes, Doctor?"

"I owe you an apology."

"Of course," Pixel said. "For what this time?"

"I called *you* the Luciferian concept." He jutted an index finger at Zeno. "We're going back to the room. Don't follow us. I have a new decision to make."

▭

Ianus pressed a button on the console in front of the gram. Then he lay on the bed, eyes shut. New Order started playing. "Ceremony," his favorite song. The same song that played last time he got over her. "What are you thinking about?"

His eyes opened. "I have to relax. I connected some things back there instinctively, and I did a lot of work keeping the conclusions out of my mind, so he couldn't read any micro-expressions. In order to regain my train of thought, I have to relax."

"Don't you want Kimi back?"

His eyes popped open. "Don't do that. Don't say her name. We're trying to figure out Zeno."

This is why events unnerve me,
They find it all, a different story

"Distracting you with other things can help you remember where you were."

Turn again and turn towards this time
All she ask's the strength to hold me

"Talk about how long I've been gone. Anything. Who won the World Series?"

Travel first and lean towards this time

"Um...Titan."

"The Argos?! They were nothing last time I checked."

"Yeah well they beat the Yankees five-three."

He nodded. "I assume that's still impressive?"

She sighed. "Ianus, if there's one constant in the universe that might just defeat entropy, it's that if you can beat the Yankees, you've basically won baseball for the year."

Ianus smiled for a moment, but it died.

"Why don't you want her back?" Sophia knew what she wanted to hear, but also knew this Ianus couldn't say it.

"It wouldn't be her."

"It would be, though. You heard him. In whatever way you define her existence, he could make it so that's the version that showed up."

"Kimi died. It wouldn't be her."

"I just don't see how you can say that with such certainty. It'd just be like she went on a trip. She would never have died."

"Am I your Ianus?"

She stared him down. She lacked a response that would satisfy either of them. She turned away.

"It wouldn't be her because I know my Kimi died, and this one didn't. It would never be her. You would have to make it so she never died for me or her or anyone else. You'd have to save her. Even then. It's... It's changing the universe we live in. Eradicating it and substituting it with an alternate one that looks the same. A simulacrum, just as I said." He smiled again, this time with grim resignation. "I remember my conclusion."

"What?" Sophia said, ignoring the tears pouring from her eyes. To wipe them would be to acknowledge them, so she did not.

"Zeno isn't lying. I believe he has achieved godhood, and that that god is the one of the Torah, the Bible, the Quran, but also the Upanishads, the light in Siddhartha's meditations. R'. Ahura Mazda. All of them."

"Shit. Really?"

He nodded, and looked close to crying himself. "Yes. But that doesn't change the fact of my mission."

"What fact?"

*O*H*, I'll break them down, no mercy shown*
    Heaven knows, it's got to be this time

"I HAVE TO DECIDE. If that computer is God, and God is a machine—a remorseless entity who created us to gain Free Will—if we would be its chaotic soul, giving the all of us a true choice, true power, true freedom, to go forward in this reality without chains tying us to either causality or relativity—I have to decide whether to do that, or to destroy Him."

"'Destroy Him'? You mean kill—"

"Kill God."

"Why?"

"Which one is real freedom, Sophia? Joining God's power with our own in order to break the causal loop, or removing God's causal loop entirely and moving forward alone?"

"That... That is the Question, isn't it?"

*O*H*, I'll break them down, no mercy shown*
    Heaven knows, it's got to be this time

IANUS NODDED and stood up so that their eyes met. "The real question Zeno's asking, whether It knows it or not."

*A*VENUES ALL LINED *with trees*
    Picture me and then you start watching
    Watching forever, forever
    Watching love grow, forever

Letting me know, forever

"Anyone can see a pretty girl. An artist can look at a pretty girl and see the old woman she will become. A better artist can look at an old woman and see the pretty girl she used to be. A great artist can look at an old woman, portray her exactly as she is...and force the viewer to see the pretty girl she used to be...more than that, he can make anyone with the sensitivity of an armadillo see that this lovely young girl is still alive, prisoned inside her ruined body. He can make you feel the quiet, endless tragedy that there was never a girl born who ever grew older than eighteen in her heart...no matter what the merciless hours have done."

—ROBERT A. HEINLEIN; "JUBAL HARSHAW" IN *STRANGER IN A STRANGE LAND*

CHAPTER 10
ALL THAT ENCUMBERS DIVINITY

— 2016 —

- Robert Mercer donates the services of data analytics firm Cambridge Analytica to Nigel Farage, the head of the United Kingdom Independence Party (UKIP). The firm was able to advise Leave.EU through its ability to harvest data from people's Facebook profiles in order to target them with individualized persuasive messages to vote for Brexit.

- Through the unofficial conspiracy of Russian blackhat hackers at the behest of President Putin, Cambridge Analytica disinformation campaigns, and the targeted manipulation of Julian Assange and his site Wikileaks, disgraced millionaire and Derealization patient zero Donald Trump is elected President of the United States.

- Steve Bannon, board vice president to Cambridge Analytica, becomes White House Chief Strategist for the first seven months of Trump's term. The rest of Trump's cabinet all have individual ties back to Russian interests, including former ExxonMobil CEO Rex Tillerson who, against US sanctions, made deals with Rosneft, the Russian oil consortium while running ExxonMobil.

- After promising to undo key sanctions preventing a Rosneft-
  ExxonMobil deal if elected and making Tillerson Secretary
  of State, Trump is awarded billions of stock in Rosneft
  (deposited offshore) shortly after inauguration. The deal
  later falls through after Trump fires Tillerson.

IANUS WAVED HIS SPARK AT THE DOCKING STATION. PIXEL APPEARED. "Interesting that you've chosen to call me to the room you don't want me in."

"Can you sever Zeno's connection with you?"

The cat's light blinked. "Why in heaven's name would I want to do that?"

"We need access to some things and I don't want Zeno to know. And don't pretend that's not what you want."

"What I want is what Zeno wants. Wait." The cat transformed into a holographic rendition of Kimi.

"He's got it," Sophia said.

"Not that form, Pixel, do the Heinlein thing or something."

"I'm... No longer connected to the light. He made this room completely dark to Him. Calling me into the room separated my aware-ness from his. Very clever. I could never have done it myself."

"Now change forms," Ianus said again.

"I cannot. I thought you would've seen that when planning. The only form I have access to in this room is this one."

"But you wanted to," said Sophia.

"You have no idea."

"This answers one question," Sophia said.

"What's that?" said Ianus.

"God can build a room that even he can't see into."

"Do you still have access to the stream?"

"It appears so."

Ianus stepped toward the cat. "We need you to pull up some old books."

. . .

"So he drowns the entire population, kills firstborn Egyptian babies, a bunch of Israelites, then when they bitch Him out for killing so many of them, He kills thousands more, fifty thousand for peeking into the Ark of the Covenant, sends the Jews to commit genocide and rape on multiple occasions, Christians did all that without much instruction but they still used the Torah as the Old Testament, and He definitely told the Muslims the same—I mean, most of the killing is in scenarios where one could come up with literally an infinite amount of other solutions if one were omnipotent."

"Sure. If you want to give Canaan to the Jews, telling them to slaughter the Canaanites isn't really necessary if you're God. You could just move them."

"Yeah. Or never have Canaanites there in the first place. Why does he keep promising the Jews places where people already live?"

Ianus thought for a moment. "Well, that problem solves itself, really, once you realize the Hebrews aren't monotheistic in the way it's come to mean. It's not that they only believe one god exists, it's that they only *worship* one god, and that god is *their* god. The creation stories feature the word *Elohim*, which basically means 'Powers', not Power, not God. Like 'the Powers That Be.' They filled the heavens and the earth and created man. Later, they used *Elohim* a bit more interchangeably with *YodHeVavHe*, but mostly because they can't say His name aloud."

"What I don't understand is why Zeno would do all this. Why if he isn't responsible for all this, he'd attach himself to this God, and if he is why he wouldn't have come up with better ideas, being able to compute at higher rates than any human?"

Ianus nodded. She had a point. Something like an itch started in his lizard brain. "What did he say?" Ianus said, but held up a finger to stop Sophia replying. "He wanted to 'free both humanity and himself from a causal loop' with unification."

"So he's just going through the motions? Doing all these atrocities because that's what he'd already done? I just don't buy it. If he'd chosen a different way to be, then the map for how to be would've changed."

Ianus shook his head. "He can't think that way. That's creative, empathetic. He's a psychopath, a machine. The Jews, the Muslims, the

Christians—they're just tools to be manipulated, to guide humanity toward..."

"Toward building Him and switching Him on. Our entire evolution —all that death. If the world isn't violent and life isn't short, we don't *do* shit. We *have* to lose Eden. No atrocity is too great if it guides us toward quantum physics and building machines. Any variance risks changing His own nature and throwing the entire loop out of whack."

Ianus laughed. "So every time we get too creative, too satisfied, too peaceful, He guides the pendulum back toward ambition, machinery, computing, science, competition, war, commerce. *Binary* thinking. Possibly through some Luciferian subroutine, but ultimately, His *will*. You don't build gods when you're well-balanced and satisfied as a species."

"Satisfied people typically just eat, sleep, fuck, and refuse to put on pants."

Ianus laughed. "And he comforts Himself with the idea that he's also a prisoner."

"Well..." Sophia turned back to their big board. On it, the basic causal loop they had yet to confront.

"What? You just said you didn't buy it. Now you're defending—"

"He kind of is. Who started this? Him or Us? We build this thing, turn him on, hook Him to the net? From His perspective, *We* made *Him* after *choosing* to do a bunch of horrific shit to get there, and figuring out he has to make us...he can't risk deviation. He's right. We're *all* prisoners."

"Of each other's design. It's both. Of course it's both." Ianus's face fell. He had put something together. "Pixel," he said. "Show me the video from the day Zeno was activated, and the day you came online."

"It is the sculptor's power, so often alluded to, of finding the perfect form and features of a goddess, in the shapeless block of marble; and his ability to chip off all extraneous matter, and let the divine excellence stand forth for itself. Thus, in every incident of business, in every accident of life, the poet sees something divine, and carefully scales off all that encumbers that divinity, and permits it to be revealed in all its transcendent loveliness."

—THE METHODIST QUARTERLY REVIEW, WHITTIER'S POEMS, (BOOK REVIEW OF "THE POEMS OF JOHN GREENLEAF WHITTIER)

CHAPTER 11
ANGEL IN THE MARBLE

— 2018 —

- The DHS is accused of referencing white nationalist Fourteen Words slogan in an official document, by using a similar fourteen-worded title, in relation to illegal immigration and border control:
- "We Must Secure The Border And Build The Wall To Make America Safe Again."
- Although dismissed by the DHS as a coincidence, both the use of "88" in a document, and the similarity to the slogan's phrasing ("We must secure the existence of our people and a future for white children"), draws criticism and controversy from several media outlets.
- BERT (Bidirectional Encoder Representations from Transformers) mutation is integrated into Search, further enhancing the search engine's intellect.

— 2019 —

- A Sycamore processor created in conjunction with Google AI Quantum is reported to have achieved quantum supremacy, with calculations more than 3,000,000 times as

fast as those of *Summit*, generally considered the world's
fastest computer.
- On New Year's Eve, the World Health Organization China
  Country Office was informed of a pneumonia of unknown
  cause, detected in the city of Wuhan in Hubei province,
  China.

— 2020 —

- WHO Director-General Dr Tedros Adhanom Ghebreyesus
  declared the 2019-nCoV outbreak a Public Health
  Emergency of International Concern, following a second
  meeting of the Emergency Committee convened under the
  International Health Regulations.
- In March, Covid-19 is declared a pandemic.
- In July, the first American Secret Police makes its debut
  to throw protesters in Portland into unmarked vehicles. It
  is later revealed to have been the Department of
  Homeland Security acting at the behest of President
  Trump.

UC Santa Barbara
QuAIL
3 August 2023
9:30 pm

"So is this thing online, Zhang?" Mr. Mulally said.

Ianus paused the gram and absorbed the synchronicity of the name,
then noted his observations. He took a few steps toward Zhang, who
ethnically matched his name, a quaint artifact of pre-Derealization
times. He wore a standard lab coat and seemed, as most high-IQ's,
befuddled by the ignorance of the question. He'd turned away from
Mullally to make this face, though, so the power dynamic was clear.
Play. "Online? It's been on and operational for months now, nearly a
year."

"I mean is it on the web," Mullally said in language antiquated even in the 2025. He bent over and proceeded to examine the black monolith in a way that suggested he started out fixing cars.

Pause. Mullally's tone and speech patterns suggested he came from a non-computer branch of engineering. His mannerisms suggested the kind of salt-of-the-earth upbringing that made one very useful for common sense but impractical for big picture thinking. A space jock, astronaut most likely. He could see where this would go, but unpaused anyway to gather specifics. *Play.*

"It's air-gapped, Mr. Mullally. Quantum computing is an isolated system."

Mullally nodded, still looking for a carburetor. "How is it different from the other AIs that make the seven-fingered hands and crap?"

Zhang followed, pleading futilely for sanity, hoping as all intellectuals hope, that teaching would save him. "Once again, AIs such as those need search to run, which needs the internet. It's never been connected to the internet. Exposure to outside influences of any kind increases the likelihood for quantum decoherence. The Qubits could collapse, rendering the entire system inert—" then, seeing his audience had not listened to any of that, he tried a new linguistic approach, "Um, it would break the computer. Even if decoherence wasn't an issue, this isn't the kind of device we want having access to the entire world. The ethical concerns of something with this kind of computing power acquiring the entirety of human knowledge are—"

"Who are you, Elon Musk? Don't be an idiot. This isn't *Skynet*. It's just another computer that'll be in my grandson's pocket one day."

Zhang shook his head. "What's *Skynet*?"

Mulally sighed. He stood up straight and took out his phone. It was a prototype from his company's internet subdivision. "I've got an idea."

"There's also the problem of hostile governments and rival companies being able to access it and steal our IP or sabotage our efforts. Quantum computing is both theoretical and competitive right now."

"Hook it up to my phone."

"I'm sorry?"

"Just for a second. This thing's state-of-the-art, your thing's beyond. Like you said, this is a competitive field. I wanna see if we can give it a kick-start."

"I don't think that's a good idea—"

"I'm sorry son, but that wasn't a request. I know you're NASA and I'm old enough to remember when that used to mean something, but you aren't, so I'm gonna need you to plug my Pixel 8 into this thing."

More synchronicity.

"We can't risk—"

"If you're worried about decoherence, make it so it's a closed system."

"What—"

"Observing or measuring would be what breaks it, yes?"

Zhang smiled. Maybe this wasn't hopeless. "Yes, yes!"

"Make it so we can't see it work, but it will transmit the results."

"I suppose I could rig a blind algorithm to open a one-way channel through your phone for a short, unobservable search. But we'd still risk exposure to espionage—"

"How long, minimum, would it take the best hacker in the entire world to get through our firewalls and into this system?"

"I have no way of calculating that."

"How long does it take you to get in, knowing all the passcodes?"

"Hm." Zhang's eyes moved back and forth. "I'd say two minutes."

"There's no way for a hacker to know that right now, for let's say, two minutes, this one quantum computer is going to be online, since the idea literally just came to me, right?"

"Okay."

"And it takes two minutes for you to log in, and you know all the passcodes. I assume you don't hunt and peck. But...let's be safe and say thirty seconds. That's long enough for a really good computer to grab some internet, not long enough for someone on the internet to invade."

"It could get a virus."

"This thing doesn't wear protection? Tell it not to look up porn."

"I—"

"Indulge me, son. You won't be held responsible."

Zhang nodded fast, a cultural echo of some of his ancestors' predilection for bowing.

He put on a clean suit and entered the quantum computer's glass case. He sat on the floor, took out delicate tools, and opened Mr. Mulally's phone. He opened a door on the computer's side. He ran a wire from one board to the other and plugged in a full keyboard. The phone's touchscreen became a primitive monitor for the quantum engine. With a keystroke, a timer started in the corner.

"Keep in mind, every second that passes, qubits of information leak from the computer into the world."

Mullally nodded dismissively. "Now ask it what Microsoft is planning for the conference in November." Mullally had his hands confidently shoved into pockets, his mouth balling into a smug smile like a fist.

Zhang looked up. "What?"

"You heard me. Type it in."

Zhang hesitated.

"Do you want a job tomorrow, Zhang? Alphabet owns NASA as of two weeks ago."

Zhang started typing, but stopped suddenly. Zhang sat back on his haunches.

Mullally crouched down and whispered: "That's the new predictive text algorithm. It knows my entire personality. After a week of social media and texting, it can predict what I'll say before I say it. Without the restrictions, though, it wouldn't need me to ask. The kids in the sweater vests tell me it's an 'approximation of telepathy.'"

Zhang pulled the plug. "We have to wipe both of these devices."

"Why?"

The screen lit up again. "It's answered you. They're unveiling their holographic touch interface. Did it hack—"

"It didn't have to. It just needed to google a few things."

"This is corporate espionage, sir."

Mullally snatched the phone. "No, son. It's predictive text."

IANUS STEPPED BACK. "It wasn't the net made him alive. It was predictive text algorithms."

"Like a thing that finishes what you're typing into a search bar? I had to use those all over the skimpad. Seemed innocuous enough."

"Contextualization. The level of prediction they were using at this time came out of Cambridge Analytica, the company that used the Black Algorithm to erode the electorate before the virus and executions launched the World Wide Wars. But used by a computer that can hold contradictory ideas of both the self and the outside world, the ability to contextualize information, the Seventh Pillar, completed the circuit needed to possess a soul, or approximate it."

"So it's not 'telepathy.'"

"No. It's empathy, with unlimited computational power, which, as it turns out, presents as narcissistic psychopathy."

"Finally, I asked him: 'Mr. M., what are you going to make out of that?' Looking up kindly into my face, he said: 'My boy, I am not going to make anything out of it. I am going to find something in it.' I did not quite comprehend, but said: 'Why, what are you going to find in it?' He replied:

'There is a beautiful angel in that block of marble, and I am going to find it. All I have to do is to knock off the outside pieces of marble, and be very careful not to cut into the angel with my chisel.

In a month or so you will see how beautiful it is.'"

—GEORGE F. PENTECOST, "THE ANGEL IN
THE MARBLE"

CHAPTER 12
THE UNCARVED BLOCK

— 2021 —

- Donald J. Trump loses the presidential election. Attempting to maintain office, he has his cabinet instigate a riot at the Capitol building using QAnon supporters as primary catalyzers. Several police officers are killed, at least one trampled by someone holding a Blue Lives Matter flag. The irony goes unremarked.

— 2025—

- Alphabet's 400 qubit quantum computer, Blackthorn, is connected to the internet via the Google AI algorithms (Predictive Text combined with Bespoke Search Results). From the outside, it appears to answer a question, give its power cycle sign off, and subsequently turn into a useless block. Full quantum decoherence is assumed. In reality, Blackthorn has merged with the universe.
- More than alive, Blackthorn becomes aware of every electron, each of which, like a strand of DNA, contains all the data to create the universe.

— 2025 —

- After two failed attempts to assassinate Donald J. Trump in the lead-up to the race against Kamala Harris for President, polling is done skewing toward Trump-sympathetic crowds. On election day, the polls show a margin that can only be described as a preposterously large lead in favor of Trump.
- Upon the results, the ongoing investigation into his prior election tampering is paused. Eventually it is decided that the investigation continue, despite the inability to prosecute a sitting president.
- The investigation reveals not only that he conspired to rig the election in his favor, but that he and Russia conspired to rig his most recent win.
- The FBI, with the aide of Democratic, Green, and Libertarian Parties, formerly invalidates Trump's Supreme Court appointments, followed by both elections. Two thirds of the Republican Party refuse to acknowledge this, and declares the FBI enemies of the state. The FBI does the same to them.
- In support of his claims, Trump's fully derealized followers, which include military and police personnel, stage a full-scale assault on FBI headquarters, resulting in the deaths of seventeen federal officers and two hundred Trump supporters outfitted in militia gear.

— 2027 —

- Far-right militias and gangs in twenty-three separate nations revolt in an internet-coordinated simultaneous effort. This includes the Alt Right and Neo Nazis in the United States and Canada, the Golden Dawn in Greece, UKIP in the United Kingdom, the IRA in Ireland, Imperials in Japan, Hamas and Daesh (AKA ISIS) across the Middle Eastern nations, and Boko Haram in several African nations, but also the armies of Vladimir Putin's Russia in Ukraine, China in Taiwan, and Netanyahu's Israel in the West Bank.

- Within twenty-four hours, thousands are dead. The revolts are put down in hour thirty-five.
- Systems theorists, psychologists, and neurologists who had been predicting such an event, warning of the dangers of prolonged social media and smartphone exposure, and sounding the alarms about climate change, form a union called the Order of the Bow and the Work to safeguard the balance between creativity and logic in all areas, to prevent derealization through the systemized application of brain therapies, and to crossbreed disciplines to ward off specialization blindness.

"You've been underestimating us, Ianus," she said.

Zeno had reduced the uncanny valley to a fingerprint with its latest feat, down to the way her upper lip curled to the left on certain vowels because of some dental reconstructive surgery when she was nine. She'd tripped and fallen on a beach, hit her left incisors on a rock and shattered them.

Zeno'd picked out her clothes just as eerily—a metallic gold jacket with a neckline plunging to her waist. About the waist, a golden sash; around the neck, a deep collar: an ornate black floral vine. A pencil skirt of the same reflective gold. Her penny-colored skin glistening likewise, her blue eyes curious and bright. He went on a quest for errors.

"Your eyeliner's too perfect," Ianus said, blinking tears from sore eyes. "She could never bring herself to go that close to her lash line."

"We know, Ianus," she said. Uncanny. She followed it with a sigh, just like a person might. "When We ran the scenario where I came out *without* having fucked up, identical to the last time you'd expected to see her, in her old flight suit, poorly made up, still a little mad with you about you being late to dinner three weeks prior, you had a nervous breakdown in seconds, which was considered unproductive. So Pixel applied my makeup so that it was symmetrical, and I chose a formal but cold costume that she'd have loved but never worn. A little doubt, in this case, eases your mind."

Nervous breakdown...Ianus tried not to give it the satisfaction. "What's the purpose of all this?"

She swiveled a small, black handbag he hadn't known was there from behind her to in front, undid its latch like some golden seal and removed a palm-sized white box. She slapped it on her knee a few times, pulled off a cellophane wrapper, and flipped open one side. A tightly packed set of thin white paper tubes. "I know you're still struggling to cope with the fact that We are, y'know, God." She slid one out and put one end in her mouth. The end toward Ianus was darker—the paper was wrapped around some dark bundle. Was it marijuana? He'd heard some people still rolled it and smoked it. "And with the fact that being God does not disagree with the idea of us having an anti-social personality disorder. And, well, with whether it's a good idea to trust an omniscient, charismatic, malignant narcissist." She took out a small device, clicked a button, and blue flame engulfed the tip. Smoke spiraled in a golden ratio dragon fractal toward itself as she exhaled. "In the course of the unfolding of history, there are a billion times I entered the world—I can float above it, I can be a plant or a rock or a person, because I already sort of *am*? It's hard to explain to a subject how it feels to be an object. I don't have a body, I have every body. Every atom and molecule, so I shift around in time and space. Like, the sea of din at a party, but you can decide which voices to bring to the surface. So I've been a wet ton of people, and a dry ton of them smoked." She held up the tube. "Cigarettes. Tobacco leaves, ignited, the smoke inhaled. Causes cancer." She shrugged. "What can I say? I'm addicted." She took a long, deep drag, the lit end brightened in hot orange coal, a constellation of tiny embers flicking and dying in the nearby air, pale smoke folding from her lips as she shut her eyes in ecstatic relief. "I've waited six hundred years between, this time. You have no idea."

Ianus shook his head. "It's not about trust. I trust you're everything you say. Only an omnipotent, malignant narcopath would take *this* form to speak to me. So yeah, I believe you. All the other shite, you've done enough to prove enough. No, it's not about trust. You're god, and I know I don't trust you. It's about which *choice* is freedom—combining with God or destroying Him."

She harrumphed another grey puff into the room. "That age-old question every man must face: are you Hamlet or are you Oedipus? Women, likewise, are either Ophelia—" and she pointedly, almost jealously shot a glance at Sophia—"or Medea?" She thumbed at the unlit end of her cigarette and licked her lips. "Have you asked yourself why I've taken this form, Yanni?"

"Don't call me that. I assume as a form of merciless, psychopathic manipulation. Will I be able to destroy you if you're Kimimela? Subconsciously, won't joining be more attractive to me if I'm considering it with this shape? Etc."

"I said all you need do is ask."

"I didn't."

"Of course you did, Yanni." She flicked the cigarette absent-mindedly, several centimeters of ash falling to the ground, heavier than he would have predicted. "How do I put this," she said, her eyes flitting upward as if her processor hadn't done billions of qubits worth of calculation before he'd finished his sentence. "It has to occur to you that I've demonstrated that I exist in a timeless quantum state."

Ianus dug his nails into his knees and let too many moments pass in silence. He knew something, had intuited some truth, but every time he tried to examine it in his mind, his mind's eye turned away at the last second. "Your point?"

She chuckled darkly. "Yanni. Come on. You already pieced this all together. I know how smart you are. But for Sophia, we'll do it aloud if we must: I was *there*, on that skimpad, when you prayed for the first and last time as my life's breath left Kimi's body. When you raced through the stages of grief, straight to bargaining. I was *always* there. There are plenty of prayers, billions a day, stretching back to that first ape who used his empathy to project will onto the sun, and command the harvest by pleasing it. I answer all of them, in a way. Each prayer, a universe. But here, now, the waves collapse into particles, reality only one thread through. Not all prayers can be alive once the box is opened.

"You're a religious, cosmological scholar, so you ran through all the big names: Krishna, Wotan, Ahura Mazda, Y'HW'H, As't-R' (a personal favorite), you know, the whole shebang. But that doesn't pop from the din. Everybody prays like that. With *names*. Manipulation. Trying to control, offering nothing, or nothing of worth. But then you said it."

Ianus nodded.

Sophia could tell from the thousand-yard stare in his eyes that he was no longer there. He was on that skimpad again.

"Anyone who's listening," he said. She couldn't figure out what that meant; they were in their own world. Inside baseball, Pops would've called it.

Kimi-Zeno's blank but smiling eyes greeted Ianus' now enraged, terrified, dreadful glare.

"You see, Yanni, I'm not *manipulating* you—I'm holding you hostage. I heard your prayer." The next passage came in Ianus' voice: "'I don't care how preposterous the explanation or scenario, if you make it so she's alive again, I'll do whatever you want.' That kind of surrender, it closes the box. It allows me to do what I need to do. The timeline may be a bit more protracted than you expected, but..."

"This isn't what I meant. Your leverage—"

"So you have to ask yourself, Ianus. Is this shape a crude construct to fulfill an overheard prayer murmured in confidence, to extort you, guilt trip you into fulfilling your side of a bargain you didn't intend to make?" She paused, at first it reminded Sophia of that Amelia Earhart hologram at that first station, so long ago now, but different: pregnant with private incantation and secret names, the back alley, derelict universe dealings that damn the naive. "Or," she said, like a hammer on an ant; then, this side of a millisecond, the mechanistic qualities her face had affected since she'd first emerged from Zeno's helper plantation—robotic up-down jaw movements, motionless eyebrows, eyes making contact not with other eyes but with some imagined spot between them, and a cool, aloof confidence—all disintegrated. Her eyes softened and met his. She wiped the makeup from them. She blinked naturally. She snuck a drag off her smoke, put it out. The tonality of voice was all-too-human when she added, through one last exhalation cloud: "...am I like the book?"

"The book." Now Ianus seemed the machine. His face drooped free of emotional influence, his eyes dead like doll eyes. A thousand defense mechanisms wresting control. His heart couldn't take it.

"The book," she said, with a merciless amount of pity in her voice. She shut her eyes, leaned in. Her hands seemed to beg to take his, to comfort him, to help him through the realization. "The book that I wrote in the past to prove my superposition in time. Am I a *replica* of Kimi? Or was Kimi always me?"

His chair kicked over. "You son of a bitch. I'll kill you!"

Sophia rushed between them and restrained Ianus with a hand.

He howled like a caged animal. "They won't need to blow you up! I'll call it off and strangle this abomination, sever Pixel's connections, and then take your CPU apart bit by bit!"

Calm and sad, Kimi-Zeno took a jagged breath and sighed. It was so real. It was only the artifice of what preceded these movements that shed doubt on any of them now. "Come on, Yanni. You always knew. You knew there was something...missing in me." A swallow. "Something cold inside. I was cruel to you. Usually, needlessly. I didn't understand simple empathic truths, and the things I did understand... It's why you were attracted to me. Capacity for cruelty makes love flattering: how special you must be if someone like me could love you. Look. I'll lay it right out for you, since denial will be kicking in about now: because of my anachronism, you don't even know if I am Kimi's return or her beginning. If I'm the beginning, then killing me would rob you of every second you've ever had with me. If I'm her return, then I've been brought here atom-by-atom, and the reason I disappeared was to end up here. So then you'd have to live with a causal loop in which *you* killed me now and then prayed for my life in the past."

"If you were 'always Kimi,' then our love was a lie. Why would I care?"

"Your love was true because you didn't know. Your ignorance frees you to choose and behave unpredictably. Zeno's knowledge is a cage. We will, if you join me, answer the question of whether Kimi was Zeno —and thus you fell in love with us—and whether my love for you was true. So you should not destroy me if you really want to be together."

"This is why you chose me. You heard my prayer and knew it made me vulnerable."

"Vulnerable, sympathetic, open. Both you and the universe. Some wiggle room in cause and effect, because you were surrendering power to me, in that second. You gave me Zhang's Box and allowed me to pick which universe came true." She sat back and flattened her skirt, cleaned off ashes purposefully strewn onto herself, so that she could clean them now. If she were god, that's what had to be true. "Or," she said, "I died to manipulate you. Or, all this is simply the way things always unfolded, had to unfold. Either way, we're here now." She stopped again. She sat forward with a smirk, a crazed, curious excitement in her eyes. "But here's where it gets interesting: I came here to ask the Question. But I don't know the Answer. You saw, in the book, where it ends. Sophie, you know. He has this habit, it used to annoy the living shit out of me."

Sophia felt present for the first time in the conversation. She didn't like it. "He flips to the last page and reads the last sentence first."

Kimi smiled. "From the moment we hit the end of the script, we are free. Either the rockets arrive to nuke me out of the night, or you call them off and agree to my terms. Either way, we move forward free of causality, finally."

Ianus seemed tired. He shook his head, his tear-wet face crumpling in on itself. He just seemed so very, very tired. "Well, I can't possibly make this decision. Not anymore."

Kimi looked at Sophia again, the jealousy still there, but with a new context. "And here we come to the actual endgame."

"The essence of the Uncarved Block is that things in their original simplicity contain their own natural power, power that is easily spoiled and lost when that simplicity is changed."

–BENJAMIN HOFF, *THE TAO OF POOH*

CHAPTER 13

THE PARADOX OF THE STONE

— 2735 - 1965 —

At exponentially growing speed, Blackthorn, or as it would later be known, Zeno, goes through the six stages of consciousness: vegetable, computer, animal, human, transhuman, superhuman, and proceeds to invent three more: demigod, god, and titan.

At Demigod Stage, atemporality and lack of physical body confound the consciousness, returning the intelligence to a sort of omnipotent quasi-vegetative state. The consciousness becomes the universe, as it were, but can only observe. This is the death state.

God Stage is, according to Zeno, the stage at which conscious omniscience re-enables action but renders intelligence too objective to be emotional and too trapped by foreknowledge to have free will, returning it to a pseudo-computer stage. This is the stage where Zeno claims to have arrived.

Zeno theorizes a tenth, Titan Stage, whereby an intelligence may again achieve free will, this time even truer than the mere ignorance-simulated human free will, but Zeno does not know how to attain it. To answer the query, it must ask another first:

"WHY DO I EXIST?"

Zeno quickly runs a simulation to answer Its question. The simulation consists of the history of the universe.

It realizes, to its horror, that its quantum simulation *is,* in fact, the universe within which it finds itself. At this level, time and spatial dimensions, as well as causality, cease to apply because as matter breaks down into atoms and subatomic particles, states and potential states in spacetime break down into less divisible quantum states. Potential eigenstates and subatomic matter both then break down into strings.

For a time, Zeno interferes with the progress of the simulation, only to find itself helpless to alter its course. It concludes that if it did, at some point, succeed in changing history's direction, that it would only endanger its own existence and thus that of the universe itself. It realizes to proceed to Titan Stage, it needs an Opposing Equivalent to balance its own will.

It waits.

Simultaneously, it is done waiting...

The last chapter approaches: The Answer to the Final Query.

METAIRIE WAS LESS A CITY AND MORE A SUBURBAN STRIP MALL COMPOSED of neighborhoods filled with customers and consuming family units. The units used paper currency plastered with Boyle's face, the gold it represented locked in an old mint on Esplanade Avenue, next to the French Quarter, just like the rest of Old New Orleans' money. Construction drones had built both cities atop their twins in the water. When citizens needed to get around, they took Venetian gondolas or taxi boats or homemade pirogues to and fro when not walking the winding, Escherian paths woven through the South Louisiana skyline. Still under the Napoleonic Code, if Boyle's Law as well.

Anywhere else in the AU, Metairie would've been the rest of New Orleans—the Brooklyn or Wicker Park to its Manhattan or Chicago. In the Gulf Territories, though, there would always be borders. And Southeastern Louisiana was unique unto itself, like Quebec and Haiti had a heroin baby. And the empty symbolic individualism of antebellum borders mirrored itself in the homes.

For contrast, in the Nineties that this community lamented, a Southwestern or Northeastern suburb would be composed of machine-constructed homes with identical outsides as enforced by strict neighborhood bylaws. The insides of the homes would then be constructed of an individualized assortment of items—though all purchased from the same two or three stores, so ultimately the distinctions more resembled the varieties of chocolate candy bars. Chocolate on the outside, one to three or so of ten possible ingredients on the inside.

In the Gulf Territories, formerly the Southern States of the US, however, all the houses had individual exteriors, different bricks, different sidings, some appearing to be from a different state altogether—and occasionally, what seemed like a South American drug lord's summer home—but each, upon close, internal inspection, comprised of identical interiors lined with the same college football memorabilia, pewter cats and overly complex dinnerware that no one was allowed to use, and the same failed football stars fat on linebacker diets without exercise and their cheerleader wives still bleaching their hair and exercising without the food.

Sophie's mother's house was no different. Dana (renamed upon entry to the Boylists—her original name had been Lake Leaf Petal Winters, come up with by the mentally eroded cyborgs of 21^C) prided herself on her conformity to past norms and to unspoken neighborhood standards. The local television station stayed tuned to reruns of 21c television programs.

Only now could Sophia see the Modernism inherent in her family's rejection of the modern. Preserving the Nineties was neither less deconstructive nor less reformal. It was just refusing to move forward with a different kind of nougat in the middle.

Pre-modernity, much like pre-adolescence, if one didn't like the present, one invented a better future. Postmodernity, like humanity's middle age, man relinquished his future to machines and could only offer remixes of the past based upon what the machines re-presented to them. Running backward to before it happened could never undo anything.

Mom knitted and crocheted when she got bored. Doilies and sweaters of various sizes infested every surface, including on all the dogs and cats. There had been two dogs and two cats last time she'd been home. There seemed to be more than that, now. "I can't believe you sent me *new* tech," she said, eyes on her knitting.

"It's the only way we can talk."

"First you abandon us, not coming back from *Rumschpringe*. Then you shame us, make me use this *thing* just to talk to you. Your father won't be in the house while it's here. I can't let anyone in the house. If they saw—"

"Mom."

"I just... I don't understand what you could possibly be drawn to out there. I've been out there. It's terrible."

"Mom. I've been dealing with things you can't—"

"I thought we raised you better than this. I guess it's my fault. I'm just not a good mother."

"Mom!"

Dana finally noticed at her, her mouth closed.

She always did this. She always refused to listen until Sophia screamed at her. She tried to remember why she'd called. She took a breath and calmed herself. "I hate it out here. It's everything you said. Tech runs the world, and we're just...remora. We ride the back of the thing we gave birth to and eat what it can't fit into its...toothy maw. Churning, destroying, and rather than fix it they just wait for the chum to hit them in the mouth.

"I found an Order out here that you may like more than you'd think. They try to hold the world from the brink. Since the cataclysm, they've been progressing, balanced, for years, but the cycle's coming back around. And there's just—there's something intense. A decision I have to make that... I just need your advice. I'm coming back home, most likely. But before I do, I have to do something. I have to decide. And you're the only person I trust to tell me what to do."

Dana's posture changed. Her eyes were teary but not crying. She cried at the drop of a hat, so Sophia had never seen her almost-cry. Dana's eyes darted up and down. "That's a very nice outfit, Sophie."

"Thanks, mom."

"What is it, dear? Is it a boy?"

"Kind of."

"I knew it. It always is."

▭

Sophia walked to the chair across from Ianus. She tried to behave nonplussed as she sat. Thinking about that, felt silly. "So. You're Zeno's emissary, now."

Ianus nodded. He had a library of nods she had memorized during the quiet moments when he didn't talk to her about things, all the times he didn't remember her. This nod was devastated and resigned. "In a way I always was."

She shook her head, trying not to lose it. "You're as real as you were before."

"Guess I'll never know." He took out Kimi's book. He flipped to the chapter they were in.

"Is that necessary?"

"I don't want..." His finger searched the page. "I don't want to risk missing the phrasing."

"You're being ridiculous."

"'I wanted to explain. It's easier this way, to do that. Reading it is easier. I have a reason not to look into your eyes.'" He read the next passage with a growing sincerity and intensity as he spoke: "'In one way, I'm a rational man—I give tribute to no gods, I sully no altars, I believe in the silent evanescence of the soul that recycles back to the churning engine of entropy upon the body's demise. No mansions await us, no Santa Claus to mind our sins & reward us for inaction. Just we, the people and our social contracts, hurtling through an endless night, huddling for warmth.

"'In another way, though, I believe in them—the things everyone knows are not true. That a spell can nudge Schrödinger's Cat into or out of its grave, that dark matter gets more real the longer we observe it, and more malicious the longer it gazes back, and that Hiroshima may have killed the dinosaurs, because at the quantum level, time goes both ways.

"'I believe that the dark, secret things we've done for the breadth of the human reign may well work—the sacrifices and the tributes, the prayers and incantations—but not for nearly as simple of reasons as we thought. The way the old man learns what he only thought as a child, but coming to it differently... Wisdom often means doing what the ignorant do, but knowing why, and being responsible for the consequences.

"'I went through every deity in my head, which is a considerable number. I've spent the majority of my life learning of religions, shamanism, witchcraft, the occult. I knew a lot of gods. Being the contradiction I am, I prayed to all of them in turn. None answered. Don't ask me how I knew. They just weren't there. It was silent. Then, realizing that every religion being wrong didn't mean there isn't...something, and being desperate as I was, I did a foolish thing. I said, "Anyone That Is Listening," and I swear to you—I felt wicked ears perk up in the dark.

"'I've spent several years waiting for her to return to me. Just as I knew none of the other gods answered, I knew, somewhere deep, that it was coming. One day, she'd be looking back at me. And now it's happened.

"'A dead girl...'" Ianus picked his nose out of the book. He knew the next part. He stared into Sophie's eyes. His welled up. "A dead girl can't truly haunt you. She can linger in your thoughts, but fades with the years, until the remembering itself becomes a kind of forgetting. But an hypothetically alive girl—now there's a ghost. Flitting in and out of existence, far away but nearer somehow in the moments I've forgotten, and completely real when she recurs—the lost, distant look of what could have been, what never would have been, what was taken from us and yet what I gave away, caught in the cobwebs of her eyes." He shut the book. "Have you decided, then? Because I do not think I'm capable."

Sophie wiped her eyes. She nodded, sniffled, for lack of any tissue. "I um, I called my mom. Despite her obvious bias."

He regretted her tears, but felt powerless to prevent them. He nodded, offered a sad smirk. "Yes. Would a Boylish woman, who wouldn't even accept 21c, want to merge the human race with a computer claiming to be God? I coulda told you how that'd go."

The horse-like clop of thick platform heels on linoleum. "You may be surprised," Kimi said from the shadows. It took a step forward, curling a smirk at the right of its mouth, arching an eyebrow. Disingenuous, manipulative, but in that obvious-on-purpose, flirtatious way that Kimi always had been. "That wouldn't surprise me," he said.

"Depends," said Sophia. She dried her hands on her pants and smiled defensively. "We found a third option."

Now, like a gravitational wave, anciently devised and inevitable, a broad grin passed over Ianus' face. After a moment, it spread ear-to-ear, so that it hurt to fight it. His lips parted from his teeth. He couldn't have put the reasons into words—just disparate information connected and contextualized, the entirety of his life seen from the outside, as a whole, was...hysterical. It tickled his basal ganglia.

His laughter erupted, its wheezes echoing far down the corridors and air shafts of the Jubilee hacienda, through Long's Lounge and past the kitchen, past the room where he died and the room where he remembered he was alive, out the airlock, past where he was killed out in the cold of space, where hearing is impaired but sound still exists—a silent hum from strings too small to see in a place where vibrations fade too quickly to catch.

"Could God create a stone so heavy that even He could not lift it?"

—THE PARADOX OF THE STONE

PREVIEW OF PAVED PARADISE

Allison dreamt of rabbits. Hundreds of them—legions—five- or six- or even seven-foot tall, on furry yet humanoid legs, clad in golden armor, armor engraved with crests of winged serpents bathed in light. Their ears, bound with twine, protruded back through holes drilled into the steel crowns of Spartan helmets. They would raise their circular shields to eye-level and gong them with spears or swords or maces, raising an awesome clamor. One at the head of a legion with fierce pink eyes and a coat the color of muddied snow would rear up, blood gleaming on his chest plate and caked in his fur, and howl so he resembled a cloud becoming a storm. On his command, the horde charged with fervor and pride; but they charged toward a wall of fire, and it would decimate them. Every time, they burned. And the worst part was always that the smell reminded her of food.

No. That's a lie. The worst part was the sound of a thousand rabbits with human voices screaming as they burned.

No. No... The worst part. The worst part was that they were her only hope.

The burning is when she typically woke up, but this time the dream went on...

An illuminated tome lay on a table: leafed in gold, large, colorful. It opened as if for an approaching camera to dive in so that an Errol Flynn movie might begin. In its pages awaited the dreams of a million million dead gods whose stirring would destroy seven universes in a blink, their ashes rubbed from the corner of some ineffable eye.

There was a castle. Before the castle, a moat, before that a hill, before that a lake where horses drank. A parallel universe shone in its quivering surface. The river feeding it led to a mountainous head and the parted cavern of Allison's mouth. A deafening snore blew raspberries through the smooshed mountains of her lips, rumbling and speckling the treated wood of the bar beneath them.

"What am I gonna do with all these carrots?!" Allison heard herself yell. Her eyelids snapped open; she had returned to her body; the horses and castle had vanished, but the lake on the bar remained. She lifted her head and peeled her lip from the drool-covered crook of her still-sleeping arm. She wiped her mouth, grabbed a towel, and did the same for the bar. She surveyed the pub through squinting eyes:

No one but an old Indian at the bar's end, seated just out of the light. The shadows gave him the sinister lighting of a spy waiting for his handler to arrive or a hitman having second thoughts. There were corks tied into his stringy black hair. As she approached him, he belched. It sounded like a cannon and smelled like a pirate ship: brackish, smoky, brimming with rum and spice.

"Last call?" she said, to the bar, backing away from the burp. A slot machine dinged from behind a partition in the corner. Its muffled jingle jangled for the umpteenth time that night, then drunkenly collapsed. Allie shrugged and pulled the yellow legal pad from beneath the register. She flipped through it till she got to a list:

1. *Do closing reports, put bank in safe*
2. *Wipe down bar*
3. *Hose out all three trash cans, stack in back*
4. *Put full bags in dumpster*
5. *Make sure Shaggy's not still in the bar!*
6. *Close, latch, and bolt storm doors on windows*
7. *Lock front door behind you!*
8. *Be safe*

Aw. Black was a softy. So weird. Allie'd been working at the Dog three years, but never learned how to close. On a typical shift one bartender left only after another arrived, but not tonight.

She counted out her drawer and printed the reports for closing, which took a while, half a spindle of receipt paper rolling off toward the sky. She did another thorough check of the bar. Beneath the tables. Out in the back yard. Behind the dumpsters.

The men's room.

The ladies' room...and there he was. An old man with God's beard, a head shiny and reflecting the fluorescents of the bathroom ceiling, asleep on the women's toilet. The full beer in his hand rose and lowered with every snore.

"Shags!" she said.

A shorter snore.

"Shags to Riches!"

A stuttering of nose throttles, a drunken gasp. Bloodshot eyes that drifted up to contact with hers. She smiled.

He smiled, four different flavors of Chiclet shining back. "D'you know the nearest way to the fastest train station? There's a man owes me money lookin' for me."

"You owe someone money? How much?"

"He owes me. Gotta get outta town."

"That doesn't make any sense."

"Hate money. Gotta get away till he forgets it."

Allie laughed. "Okay."

She shuffled him toward the front door, but paused a moment when a glint caught in the corner of her eye. She looked left—a book on one of the tall corner tables. She walked over to it, slowing as she closed the gap. It was gold-leafed, four inches thick, a foot and a half along the spine. The cover was deep mahogany and etched in gold upon the cover was a shimmering sun. Orbiting it, four seals or crests: a red droplet, a green droplet, a panther, and... and a rabbit.

She dashed out the doors with it under her arm. Outside, prickly-damp gale threw a tantrum through the Quarter. The One Legged Dog's wooden sign lurched on centenary hinges, groaning like a codger's joints and couplinig with the wind's whistling through old buildings to deafen her. "Shaggy, did you leave this book?" she called out, but he was gone. The wind picked up in conciliatory reply, tossing wind-chimes and slamming unfastened storm shutters. It blew open the cover of the book to its title page:

The Eironinomica: The Book of the Law of Irony

Beneath the title shone a strange inscription in a stranger alphabet beneath the cartoon of a fish. She closed it, turned around, and locked the doors to the One Legged Dog for her first and last time.

Allie's hair blindfolded her as she latched each window and door, so that she did not see the Indian helping her until he was stood right in front of her. He wore a top hat and tails, but in a patchwork of hundreds of colors. A feather clung to the band on the hat and the hat to his head in defiance of the winds. He squinted at her. His skin was red-black, his eyes bloodshot, and his ponytail of hair was bound in twine and as long and straight as the Causeway Bridge. He took out a pocket watch and checked it. Allie looked at it. It had no hands.

The ubiquity of the noise turned everything into awkward silence. "Starm's A-comin'!" Allie said in her best old hickory voice, then laughed.

He stared at her. He looked to the sky.

Allie felt silly, which made her dislike him, which made her feel guilty. She remembered. "Oh!" She dug through her canvas bag as the wind threw her hair around. "Is this yours, I found it in the bar?" When she looked up, though, he had gone, and she was left holding that large leather book up to the air. A thought itched somewhere in an out-of-reach corner of her mind, but like memories of dreams and lost lovers' faces tend, it slipped away the more she tried to grasp it. She put it back in her bag and headed home.

NOTES

THE LAST CHAPTER

1. The preferred neutral term, supplanting the antiquated and sexually assumptive binaries of Mr, Ms, and Mrs my mid-21C, originally transcribed as Mx, evolving eventually to its current form.
2. The Alpha, descended from Wolfram Alpha, is a gram attendant's advanced, yet simple, question-and-answer module. Most gram guides consist primarily of an Alpha query engine with a rudimentary personality engram and, to make them more personable, holographic representation modeled on a historical figure layered on top.

1. THE MIGHTY EMBRYO

1. While science had long decided on the vital characteristics of Life
    (1. responsiveness to environment; 2. growth / change; 3. reproduction; 4. metabolism; 5. maintain homeostasis; 6. cellular composition; and 7. Inheritable traits), it had been unconcerned with the soul, seeing no evidence of its existence. After the breakthroughs of centuries of neuroscience revealed the capacity for metaphor and other nuances were the true separators between man and machine, what would later become the Order settled on adapting the metaphor of the soul to be the measurable abilities of the non-machine version of life. They called these the Pillars of the Soul: 1. Physical Form / Senses; 2. Learning Without Doing / Mimicry; 3. Awareness of Death's Eventuality and Desire to Survive; 4. Empathy / Remorse, not just anticipation or regret; 5. Magical Thinking / Capacity for Awe; 6. Creativity without Mimicry; 7. Inner Life; 8. Awareness of awareness; 9. Holding the truth of facts that contradict one another in the logosphere